SCIENCE & ITS LIMITS

Del Ratzsch

The Natural Sciences in Christian Perspective

InterVarsity Press
Downers Grove, Illinois
Leicester, England

InterVarsity Press, USA
P.O. Box 1400, Downers Grove, IL 60515, USA
World Wide Web: www.ivpress.com
E-mail: mail@ivpress.com

Inter-Varsity Press, England
38 De Montfort Street, Leicester LE1 7GP, England

InterVarsity Press®, U.S.A., is the book-publishing division of InterVarsity Christian Fellowship/ USA®, a student movement active on campus at hundreds of universities, colleges and schools of nursing in the United States of America, and a member movement of the International Fellowship of Evangelical Students. For information about local and regional activities, write Public Relations Dept., InterVarsity Christian Fellowship/USA, 6400 Schroeder Rd., P.O. Box 7895, Madison, WI 53707-7895.

Inter-Varsity Press, England, is the book-publishing division of the Universities and Colleges Christian Fellowship (formerly the Inter-Varsity Fellowship), a student movement linking Christian Unions in universities and colleges throughout the United Kingdom and the Republic of Ireland, and a member movement of the International Fellowship of Evangelical Students. For information about local and national activities write to UCCF, 38 De Montfort Street, Leicester LE1 7GP.

Cover illustration: Seth Shostak / Photo Researchers Inc.

USA ISBN 0-8308-1580-5
UK ISBN 0-85111-466-0

Printed in the United States of America ∞

Library of Congress Cataloging-in-Publication Data has been requested.

British Library Cataloguing in Publication Data

A catalogue record for this book is available from the British Library.

15 14 13 12 11 10 9 8 7 6 5 4 3 2 1
11 10 09 08 07 06 05 04 03 02 01 00

Contents

98295

Preface

Science, it is widely believed, speaks with authority on a broad range of matters. Many people enthusiastically welcome that authority, seeing science as representing the ultimate hope for humanity—the bright light of reason triumphant over ignorance, superstition, bigotry and human finitude. For others, however, science's claim to authority is not a legitimate claim at all, and the very real power science nonetheless wields is seen as dragging in its wake the devaluation of all that is most precious, the shattering of all that is most fragile, and the technological straightjacketing of life and hope. Perhaps most numbing, on this latter view, is science's alleged ripping through the beauty of reality and claiming to find beneath it only a temporary, ultimately meaningless, chaotic fury of blind matter and energy.

But can science really deliver on either such promises or such threats? Can it properly carry us to such heights or such depths? That depends on what science is—and is not. It depends on what its capabilities and powers really are—and are not. It depends on just how far its legitimate authority extends—and does not. Pursuing such questions plunges us deep into the heart of the discipline known as the philosophy of science. The philosophy of science is basically the study of what science is, what it does, how it works, *why* it works and what we should make of it. In the pages that follow we will be concerned with those questions as well as related questions especially important to Christians. It might seem initially as though philosophical questions connected with science would have little significance for Christians. After all, science has to do with *this* world, and this world is destined to pass away. Philosophy often seems to have little to do with *any* world—at least, philosophers are widely perceived as being out of touch with this one. So why should Christians be concerned with *philosophy* of *science?*

Whether we welcome the fact or fear it, our thinking about the cosmos in which we live, our conceptions of ourselves and our place in that cosmos, and even our simple daily routines are infused with the theories, products and often-unrecognized presuppositions of science. Some of those things lie near the core of our fundamental stances toward reality, of our daily structuring of our own existence, of the framework of beliefs, values and decisions governing the who and what of our lives. Our *worldviews,* in short, are now inescapably shaped by science. Thus anyone striving for a unified, coherent, sense-making picture of both external and internal reality must come to grips with what science is, what it says and what role it should properly occupy in our conceptual and practical worlds. Those issues need to be examined for the simple reason that the implicit worldviews most people operate with *already* contain answers to those questions—answers that have been uncritically, even unconsciously, absorbed from surrounding culture.

There are some fairly large issues at stake here. If, for whatever reason, we misconstrue science and grant it too large a role, we may, as some of its critics fear, distort or destroy some deep part of ourselves and our human meaning. If, for whatever reason, we misconstrue science and grant it too small a role, we may, as others fear, destine ourselves to crawl in regions where we could fly. And there can be even deeper issues at stake for Christians. As most Christians know, unquestioning internalization of beliefs, behaviors and outlooks from the surrounding insistently secular culture is risky. If science has become an ineradicable part of our worldviews, and if our picture of science is skewed, then other parts of our worldviews that must adjust themselves to that skewed picture are at risk of undergoing deformations of their own. That raises a further crucial question. If mistaken conceptions of science go deeply enough into our worldviews, might it even be possible for the resulting deformations to touch aspects of our religious beliefs? We had better know.

The purpose of this volume (like that of the earlier edition, *Philoso-*

phy of Science, InterVarsity Press, 1986), is to give Christians an initial understanding of what natural science is, what it can do, how and why it works, and what it cannot do. In general this volume closely follows that earlier one. However, a few parts have been expanded (e.g., discussion of Karl Popper's philosophy of science), and there have been a number of small insertions into existing chapters (e.g., discussion of postmodern conceptions of science). There have been two major new additions. The first is a chapter on Intelligent Design theory—a topic that has generated quite lively debate both within and beyond the Christian scientific community. The second is an appendix concerning disputes within the Christian community. Over the years, claims by and about science have been a significant flashpoint for disputes within the Christian community, and the conduct of those disputes has often left something to be desired. It thus seemed appropriate to include in this volume a brief discussion of principles concerning such disputes.

In the earlier volume I acknowledged debts to a number of people, and to the extent that this volume follows that earlier one, those debts—to Al Plantinga, Nick Wolterstorff, Clif Orlebeke, Dick Purtill, Gary Deason, Joan Lloyd Guest, Jane Wells and others—still stand. For the present volume, I am additionally indebted to Kelly James Clark, C. Stephen Evans, Lee Hardy, John Hare, Stephen Wykstra, Lambert Zuidervaart and other members of the Calvin College philosophy Department. Donna Kruithof not only (still) puts up with about a dozen philosophers on a daily basis but continues to provide secretarial support for projects like this one, well and cheerfully. David Van Baak, friend, colleague, weekly lunch partner for nearly twenty years and an ongoing source of wide-ranging and surprising information, merits a special thank you. I am also grateful to the Pew Foundation and to Calvin College for special research support. And as usual, the InterVarsity people—James Hoover, Andrew Le Peau and others— were delightful to work with.

The first edition of this book was dedicated to Betsy. I want to renew that dedication—after all, I'm more than a decade deeper in debt to her now.

1

Science:
What Is It?

The *philosophy of natural science is basically the study of what* natural science is, what it does, how it works, why it works and how far it works. A reasonable place to begin would be with a definition of *natural science*. However, the term has no standard, accepted definition. That might seem to be an insurmountable difficulty. How can we investigate the nature of science if we do not, strictly speaking, know what we are talking about? But such problems are not insurmountable in comparable situations. For instance, it is almost a cliché that no one can define *love*. But that does not stop us from proclaiming (often correctly) our undying version of love to select persons on Valentine's Day, and it does not keep us from marrying for love. We can often recognize instances of and characteristics of a concept even if we are unable to formulate an ironclad definition of it, and we often have a good general idea even if we cannot specify all of the details. Such is the case with the general concept of *science*.

Let us begin then by setting out some general aspects of science. In the three chapters that follow we will look at some of the major attempts to specify the details.

Aspects of Science

First of all, science (or each science) is a *discipline*. This fact implies among other things that science is in some way systematic and comprehensive; it implies that it has characteristic methods, addresses specific types of questions, advances specific types of answers and carries with it a fund of results (often changing) as well as a characteristic set of presuppositions (also sometimes changing).

Not all disciplines, however, are sciences. For instance, engineering is a discipline, but is not a science in the strict sense. Engineering is an *applied* discipline whereas the sciences are typically *theoretical*, dealing essentially with abstract entities, theoretical processes and principles, and being more concerned with understanding than with the practicalities of "how to."

But its being theoretical does not distinguish natural science from other intellectual disciplines. Philosophy, for instance, is a theoretical discipline in this broad sense. But while philosophy deals largely, sometimes almost exclusively, with immaterial phenomena and concerns, the sciences focus on material things and events. Yet concern with the natural and material does not characterize natural science alone. Theology is also deeply concerned with things and events in the physical world. In fact, God's creation of and providential governance of that world are basic theological themes. The natural sciences, however, have a different set of concerns than theology. Physical reality seems to embody a characteristic web of material structures, patterns, and systems of behaviors that define what *nature* is. Natural science seeks to see the deep contours of that web, and to the extent possible, to understand the things and events within it in their own terms, discovering *natural* explanations.

Of course, "natural" explanations can potentially come in all shapes—some of which would not strike us as genuinely scientific. Historically some "natural" explanations have been unhindered by any close connection to empirical data. But a genuine science must be in tune with facts, and we get in touch with most of the relevant facts by experience, by observation, by the senses—in short, by *empirical* processes. Genuinely scientific explanations must in some sense be subject to empirical constraints.

The empirical base on which a science rests cannot, however, be an arbitrary base. *Some* cognizance must eventually be taken of any available real data, regardless of how hard it is to square those data with one's favorite theory. Pseudoscientists sometimes pick out only those empirical data that support their theories and ignore the rest. So although a pseudoscience might rest on empirical data, the database is often preferentially skewed. A real science cannot properly be quite so self-protective. It must exhibit some degree of *objectivity* in handling the empirical data.

But not just any old connection to the empirical will do. A national sensationalist tabloid once published the theory that the wife of a famous entertainer was the descendant of aliens. A key piece of empirical evidence (nearly the only one) given in support of that theory was that the lady had slightly lower than average blood pressure. Now, lower-than-average blood pressure is indeed empirical data, but there is no earthly (or unearthly) reason to connect it with alien ancestry. Real science requires that there be some *rational* connection between explanatory theory and empirical data.

The following working definition of *natural science* incorporates what has been said thus far:

> A natural science is a theoretical explanatory discipline that objectively addresses natural phenomena within the general constraints that (1) its theories must be rationally connectable to generally specifiable empirical phenomena and that (2) it normally does not leave the natural realm for the concepts employed in its explanations.

It might look initially as though many of the characteristics of science are not present in that definition. For instance, is not science often highly mathematical? Does it not involve testing? Is it not in some sense communal? Although those terms are not used, those categories are implicitly present in the above definition. Mathematics is really one way in which *rationality* is preserved within science. Testing is one way in which the *empirical* enters into science. The public, communal nature of science is one way in which *objectivity* is fostered within science.

Those three concepts—the empirical, the objective and the rational—are key to the nature of science. As we will see, much debate in this century concerning science has been over exactly what those concepts are, exactly how they are exemplified within science, and whether all of them really can be seen in the workings of science and scientists.

Presuppositions of Science

In addition to characteristic general properties such as those discussed above, a number of philosophical assumptions characterize science. For instance, it has been historically assumed that nature is understandable. Were there no prospect of understanding nature, we would have less motivation to study it. This faith in the intelligibility of reality goes back at least to ancient Greek thinkers.

It is also a presupposition of science that nature is uniform, that processes and patterns that we see on only a limited scale (since we have not examined all of creation, nor have we seen it during its entire existence) hold universally. Were that regularity not assumed, we would have no reason to think that laboratory events observed here and now could tell us about processes in the interior of distant stars far in the past. Nor would there be any grounds for believing that causal connections discovered yesterday would still hold true tomorrow, or for believing that nature is predictable or that scientific results should be reproducible. This faith in the universality and stability of the basic rules of nature goes back at least to the ancient Greeks.

Science also presupposes that observable patterns in nature provide keys to unobservable patterns and processes. For instance, we cannot directly see atoms and other such micro-entities, yet most scientists are confident of their existence on the basis of larger-scale things that humans can see—cloud-chamber tracks and so forth. On the other end of the scale are phenomena that scientists are confident about but which are simply too big for humans to see. Scientists talk confidently about the large-scale structure of the universe and about the long-term history or future of the universe. We cannot directly follow such pro-cesses on our small temporal and spatial scale of observation, but what we can see is taken as evidence for such processes. Again, faith in that presupposition goes back at least to the ancient Greeks.

Although those (and other) presuppositions are widely accepted, the metaphysical systems that originally supported them are not, and so philosophers and scientists in this century have sought elsewhere for the necessary justifications for them. Similar concerns have arisen over the objectivity, rationality and empiricality that are thought to characterize science. Why should science have *those* properties? Some argue that the nature of science must reflect the construction of reality and that in some ways those properties of science are such reflections. Christians often take the case one step further, claiming that because science must reflect reality and because that reality is a *creation*, humans must pursue their study of nature empirically, ratio-nally and objectively.

For instance, *why must science be empirical?* Why can't we learn about the world by purely contemplative means as we sit in our recliners? Because for one thing, the world is a creation undertaken *freely* by God. Had his creating been bound by rules, then if we knew those rules, we could deduce from them what he *had* to have done and consequently what the creation had to be like. But his creating was not so tightly bound as all that. He created freely, so we must *look* to find out what nature is like. For another thing, there are many ways consistent with basic rules of human thought that the world *could* have been. We must again look to see what God has done, especially since creation is not dependent on us.

Or *why must science be rational?* Because the world is the creation of a Person who created with wisdom. We expect patterns, regularity and uniformity, and we anticipate the understandability (at least in principle) of the world and the elegance of its patterns, especially since the Creator of the order in nature also created our reason.

And *why must science be objective?* Because humans have not been successful at leaping accurately to general truths about creation from isolated, preferentially screened bits of data. We must in humility recognize that while we creatures have been given the wonderful faculty of reason, we are still finite beings, and we ought not reject whatever help nature may give us.

So the fundamental characteristics of science and the fundamental assumptions of science have some foundation for the Christian, but the secular thinker must often accept them as mere assumptions—as brute presuppositions. The Christian thus has a broader context not only for doing science but for thinking about science itself.

Besides those fundamental issues, further questions arise over the epistemological status of science. When we adopt a scientific theory concerning, say, unobservable entities such as electrons or quarks, does science give us the right to say that we *know* that those theories are true? Can science yield accurate pictures of hidden objects, mechanisms and processes? Is science universally competent? Can science discover all truth, or are there questions to which science simply cannot be made to apply? Is science our only route to knowledge? If science cannot operate in a given area, must we remain forever ignorant in that area? And what claims does science have on us? Are there ever situations in which we *ought* to reject the deliverances of science even though they seem rationally impeccable? Just how should Christians incorporate science into their world?

In the chapters that follow we will examine such questions. We will begin by seeing how such concerns are (or have been) pursued in the twentieth century.

2

The Traditional
Conception
of Science

B*y the "traditional" conception of science I refer to the general*
view dominant from the seventeenth century until the mid-twentieth
century, a view still persisting in some circles.

The seventeenth century is often pegged as the beginning of science in its modern form. During that time investigations of nature
came to have a pronouncedly different flavor than the investigations
of earlier times. That difference seemed to stem from a new insistence
on trying to let scientific theorizing be objectively and rationally governed by nature via empirical observation. The spectacular successes
of Galileo, Kepler and Newton seemed a powerful vindication of that
program, and the new conception of science—destined to become by
the twentieth century the traditional wisdom on the topic—took firm
hold. In exploring it we will begin with a generic early version and
then discuss how some details and difficulties with that conception
were worked out by the middle of the twentieth century.

The Baconian Conception

The early view of modern science came from Francis Bacon (1561-1626).[1] According to the Baconian view scientists began by collecting observational data in some purely objective manner, free of all prejudices on the topic being investigated, having no prior preferences concerning what theory should be correct and not hampered by any surreptitious philosophical or religious presuppositions. They then organized their data in some naturally perspicuous way, again without any smuggled presuppositions or constraints. Then by a process known as induction, the correct generalizations and explanatory principles emerged out of the organized data. In some cases more than one possible explanation might emerge, and then additional data could be collected to settle the issue in favor of just one of those possible explanatory principles. But at no point did presuppositions, philosophical predispositions, religious principles or any subjective constraints enter in.

In this method the three basic characteristics attributed to science were to be absolutely preserved. The lack of any presuppositions or a priori restraints on the process guaranteed its objectivity. Basing the entire process on empirical data alone guaranteed its empiricality. And the process was to be rigorously rational in depending only on the logical process of induction.

Despite its persistence in popular thought the view is seriously inadequate. The reasons are straightforward.[2] First, if data were collected simply as they came to one, with no selection principles, the result would be a collection of bits of information largely unrelated to each other and probably irrelevant to whatever one was studying. But sorting the relevant from the irrelevant inevitably involves some prior ideas about what processes are related, what causal principles might be involved and what factors are not relevant. For instance, if one is studying growth rates of trees at various altitudes, one has already decided that altitude may be a relevant factor, and one has probably also decided that whether the trees are beautiful is not relevant. Data cannot be productively collected in the absence of *all* presuppositions. Data collection is, in fact, generally guided by some theory that the scientist is interested in. (And of course, science cannot be done at all in the absence of presuppositions about uniformity of nature, the consistent operation of causal mechanisms and so on.)

Second, data do not organize themselves. What category a datum properly goes into often becomes clear only when the theory explaining that datum emerges. For example, confusion about how many different categories of heat generation there are and what they are was not resolved until the discovery of various theoretical principles concerning heat. Until that time it was not known whether heat produced in the bodies of warm puppies was an instance of something akin to combustion or not. And for centuries it was believed that solar heat was a result of combustion, making it another item in the combustion-heat category. But if data just naturally organized themselves and dictated the category into which they ought to be placed, these confusions of categorization would never have occurred. But the fact is that *scientists* must organize their data, and they do so in accordance with prior suppositions—or theories—about what is related to what, what items are of the same or distinct kinds and so on. So the second step in this inductivist scheme of science fails as decidedly as the first.

The third step (the inductive step from which the inductivist picture takes its name) fails most spectacularly of all, for the theories and explanatory principles that arise within science are products of human invention and insight, not logical results of data. There is no *rigorous logical* procedure that accounts for the birth of theories or of the novel concepts and connections that new theories often involve. There is no "logic of discovery." It takes an imaginative leap to go from a body of data to a theoretical account of that data. The data are important; they provide clues that a scientist may use. But they do not *dictate* a particular theory as the proper one or particular concepts as the appropriate ones. Theories are "underdetermined" by data.

In fact, any collection of data can support or be explained by any number of different theories, just as any collection of points on a graph can have any number of distinct lines drawn through it. Some of the lines drawn through a common set of points will be smooth and simple; some will resemble spaghetti. Similarly, some theories that explain some set of observations may be simple and elegant, while some will be messy, arbitrary or ad hoc. (We tend to accept elegant and simple theories and reject the messy ones, but that may be just a result of another of our philosophical preconceptions inherited from the Greeks, the idea that nature is fundamentally simple and elegant.) But any collection of data can be explained by many possible theories, and the data by themselves do not dictate acceptance of any single one of the theories.

In some cases of course we can only think of one theory that will explain what we see. Sometimes we cannot think of any. But that indicates something about us, not the data. Certainly in such cases the data are not forcing us in a specific direction. Thus again the inductivist view falls short. Theories do not arise automatically from data. Much less does a *single* theory emerge automatically.

So contrary to inductivist views, the situation seems to be this: when scientists collect data, they have to have some presuppositions, some idea of what is or what is not going to help this particular study. When they organize their data, they must have some views concerning what goes with what and what goes into what category. And although these views or hypotheses or theories may be suggested by the data, they are not logical consequences of the data. They are the results of creative insights on the part of humans.

As one might suspect, these criticisms of the Baconian view raise some questions for the simple objective-empirical-rational scheme. If we can neither collect nor organize data usefully without bringing prior hypotheses or theories or suspicions to the task, and if there is no strictly logical process for coming up with those theories and hypotheses, then in what sense can one hold that science is *rational?* And if those hypotheses and theories, although sometimes suggested by empirical data, are at least in part the results of subjective, inventive human processes, and if they in turn direct data collection and organization, then isn't the *objectivity* of science compromised? And if the empirical base only suggests, then just what is the relationship of scientific theory to empirical data? In other words, just how *empirical* is science after all?

By the early to middle part of the twentieth century some widely accepted answers to those questions had been hammered out. We will look first at the general sweep of the answers contained in the "traditional" (or "received") conception of science and then look at one specific version of that traditional view.[3]

The Traditional Conception: Rationality

One of the most profound methodological revolutions within philosophy began with the development of modern symbolic logic early in this century. According to one school of thought, even mathematics was an extension of symbolic logic, and the view that rationality was to be defined within the parameters of modern logic was common. If that was correct, then science—seen as a paradigm instance of rationality—had to conform to the structure of modern logic, and the various parts of proper method had to have the same overall structure that logicians found exhibited in good arguments.[4]

Let us see how that idea worked in a few specific instances.

1. Prediction. Suppose that someone wishes to predict where a cannonball will land if fired under certain conditions. First he will need to collect some data about those *initial conditions:* the angle of the cannon, the energy generated by the charge, the mass of the cannonball, the configuration of the terrain and perhaps a few other bits of observational data. He will then apply some law, perhaps Newtonian, to the data and then mathematically deduce a result concerning where the impact will be. That result, deduced from the appropriate law, is his prediction. Or suppose that a scientist has a hypothesis about the formation of the solar system. She might then deduce from her hypothesis something about the composition of surface moon rocks, arguing that if the hypothesis is correct, then the composition would be such and such. In short, she would show that her hypothesis predicts the result in question.

In both sorts of cases predicting involves an *argument,* or *deducing* (often mathematically) a result of some principle or law. Thus prediction seems to fall well within the logical model.

2. Covering-law model of explanation. Explanation[5] was construed along the same lines. Explaining something was thought to involve showing that, given the relevant laws and initial conditions, the event in question was exactly what one would have expected—that it had to have happened given those laws and conditions. For instance, suppose that a cannonball lands beside you and you want a scientific explanation of why it landed there instead of twenty feet farther away. The proper answer, on this view, would be that given the elevation of the cannon barrel, the size of the charge and so on, and given the relevant laws of ballistics, it would naturally land just there and nowhere else. (You might of course be more interested in another sort of explanation: Just exactly what did whoever fired the thing in your direction think he was doing?) Notice that essentially the same example occurred two paragraphs back as an example of prediction. That is exactly right, because on the traditional view prediction and explanation were logically identical. Both were derivations from initial conditions and laws, hypotheses or theories. It was thought that the only real difference was that predictions were done prior to the event (as the name implies), while explanations were after the event. Thus if you could explain something, you should have been able, in principle, to predict it ahead of time given the requisite information. Both were cases of showing that some thing was the *expected* result given certain facts about the world, regardless of whether the expectation came before or after the fact.

That view is a type of *covering-law* theory of explanation. One explains something by showing that it falls under the covering of (or conforms to) some natural law.

Notice that explanation and prediction both involve use of general principles. Where do those general principles come from? One source was "inductive generalization"—the generalizing of regularities within the realm of our experiences to all of the appropriate portions of reality, including those portions beyond the realm of our actual experiences. For instance, under standard conditions water has (as far as we have ever observed) boiled at 100°C. We typically generalize that into the belief that all water, everywhere and always, has, does and will boil under standard conditions at 100°.

But that generalizing depends on an assumption that nature is uniform. If nature were not uniform, if the future were not like the past, there would be no reason to think that principles that held last week would hold next week. But the principle of the uniformity of nature is not a *provable* principle. And if explanation and prediction depend on general principles that rest on this uniformity principle, then scientific results will always be less than absolutely proven. There will always be at least a bit of ineradicable tentativeness to scientific results.

We must note, however, something deeper about these projections (projecting from the realm of our experiences into realms of the past, future or other parts of the universe that we have not directly experienced). At any given point in history our investigations of the world are quite incomplete, limited as they are to a particular region in space and time, limited by our abilities and interests, limited by our means of observing and restricted in some other ways beyond our control. Given the limitations under which we work, why should we think that the small portion of reality we know is wholly representative of the larger whole? Perhaps it is, but what *rational justification* for believing that might we have? Suppose that nature is uniform and that we have found some regularities in the small area we have studied. How might we be assured that those regularities we have seen are not simply coincidence resulting from unusual factors within the small area of our experience?

3. Hypothetico-deductive testing.[6] The answer seems to be that we cannot be *assured* of that but that we can try to skew the odds a bit more in our favor by increasing the range of our experiences. If some regularity we have observed is simply a coincidence and not a true natural regularity, then by increasing the scope of our experience we raise the chances that we will run into a case that is contrary to our coincidental regularity. And if it is indeed genuinely contrary to it, that will show that the regularity we had seen previously was simple coincidence.

This process of enlarging the range of our experiences is called testing. A scientist will be interested in some general law, theory or hypothesis (a conjecture concerning a possible natural regularity, for instance). He will know of cases where that apparent regularity is manifested and will not know of any where it fails. But is it a universal pattern? To try to find out he will examine new cases or collect new specimens to see if they fall into the same patterns as did the previous ones. If they do not, then he may conclude that what had previously looked like a universal pattern really was not; he had merely seen a limited and nonrepresentative sample. If they do, then he may become increasingly confident that the regularity is universal, although of course he still will not have *proof* that it is, since (although larger than before) his sample is still limited and possibly nonrepresentative. Some new case suggesting that his hypothesis is false (falsifying the theory) *may* turn up tomorrow—or next week, or next year.

Finding new cases to examine may be quite difficult. The scientist may have to set up special, artificially controlled conditions to try to bring about a relevant situation for observation—an *experiment*. Or she may have to wait for nature to produce the right conditions. If the study concerns typhoons, there is no recourse but to wait for the next one.

So on the basis of the principle being tested, one predicts what is to be expected in specific new cases. One then observes under appropriate conditions (natural or artificial) whether the prediction is born out. If it is not, then (on this view) the alleged regularity probably was not a real regularity after all. This is the *hypothetico-deductive* model of testing. From one's *hypotheses* about a natural regularity one *deduces* a prediction. Since any principle that leads to incorrect consequences is itself incorrect, rejecting a hypothesis because it leads to false predictions also seems to be a purely *logical* process.

The Traditional Conception: The Empirical Element

The traditional view's insistence on the empirical nature of science got worked out in a variety of ways. First of all, in the procedures important to science—prediction, explanation, testing, confirmation—the empirical element was prominent. Predictions were empirical predictions. Explanations were explanations of what had been observed. Predicted observational results were what constituted scientific tests. Theories were confirmed by positive empirical instances, and when a hypothesis was rejected, it was on the basis of empirical data. More fundamentally, data were always *empirical* data. It was those empirical data that had to be organized. And it was those empirical data and their regularities that had to be explained.

In fact it was widely accepted that nothing was scientific unless it was empirical or at least in principle subject to empirical testing.[7] Any claim that could not be empirically tested was simply not considered a part of science. Nonempirical claims might be interesting and even deeply important, but they were not science; and since science was supposedly committed to saying only what the empirical data warranted, science could make no pronouncements on those claims.

So on the traditional view the empirical nature of science was to be guaranteed by resting all the logic-constrained procedures on an empirical foundation, requiring a clear connection to the empirical of all claims within science, refusing to be drawn into discussions for which there could be no empirical decision procedure, and insisting on the empirical as the sole, ultimate arbiter of theory acceptability.

The Traditional Conception: Objectivity

The traditional view's commitment to objectivity was made explicit in a variety of ways. First, it was generally held that observation was inherently objective and neutral. No matter what one's background, training, presuppositions or favorite theories were, one still *saw* the same things as everyone else. There might be disputes over interpretations or explanations of what one saw, but the bare observational experiences relevant to science were surely the same for everyone. Those neutral, public, shared observational facts could be employed to settle disputes objectively and to objectively guide one away from incorrect theories. Since the processes were to be logical, if the observational data on which the logic operated were objective and neutral, then the results of those logical processes would likewise be objective and neutral. The neutrality of observation could then serve as the bedrock on which the objectivity of science was built and on the basis of which initially divergent views would ultimately be forced to converge. Science then would be ultimately self-correcting, since no matter where you started from, the objectivity of observation would ultimately force you away from the errors in that starting point.

Of course, scientists being (regrettably, according to some) human, some of them might let their prejudices and predispositions sway them. Some might let their subjectivity get out of control. But objectivity would still be maintained *communally* within science. Since what was fundamentally real was in some sense permanent (a view inherited from the Greeks), and since nature was uniform (a supposition necessary to science), any real scientific result should be reproducible. If the scientific *community* did not accept results unless they could be and had been reproduced by other scientists, then lapses of objectivity by individual scientists would not harm the enterprise of science since nonreproducible results would not be accepted by the community.

Further, one of the motivations behind finding a logic to all aspects of science and demanding the ultimate priority of the empirical was simply to make the structures of science such that at no point could the nonobjective gain entry.[8] There was to be no place where, for instance, philosophical or religious predispositions could exert any influence on theory selection.

Of course, the recognition that there was no logic of discovery and that, consequently, subjective human processes intruded into the process of theory invention posed a challenge. We will look more closely at that challenge and at one type of response in more detail in chapter five.

The Traditional Conception: Some Initial Implications
These components of the standard conception had a number of further implications for science. To mention just two, the hypothetico-deductive picture more or less enshrined tentativeness in the structure of science, and the neutrality of scientific fact gave rise to a particular conception of scientific progress.

As suggested earlier, any collection of observational data can in principle be explained by any number of different theories (although it is often difficult to construct many or, sometimes, even any plausible ones). Therefore, if theories can only be evaluated by their observational consequences as the hypothetico-deductive method implies, then since data underdetermine theories, there is no way in principle to ever settle conclusively on any single theory by purely empirical means. Thus experiment and testing and observation can never *prove* the correctness of any given theory.

The neutrality of scientific observation and the consequent neutrality of scientific results guarantee that the historical progress of science will be one of sequential accumulation of more and more scientific information. If scientific results are objective, they will be stable over time; thus any *real* scientific facts discovered by Galileo, Kepler, Newton and others will still be scientific facts. Of course, some things that they *thought* were scientific facts may not have been, but on this view where they were right, those facts are still a part of science. So subsequent generations of scientists have been merely correcting old mistakes and adding new scientific knowledge to the structure.

Positivism: A Major School in the Traditional View

While we have seen the general outlines of the perception of science during the first half of the twentieth century, the picture is not yet detailed. Different schools of thought filled those out in various ways. One way, known as "logical positivism," or simply "positivism," was by far the most influential. In the early part of this century the leading figures of this movement were members of a group of philosophers, scientists and mathematicians in Vienna known as the Vienna Circle.[9]

Although this movement was characterized by a philosophical extremism on the issues of rationality, objectivity and empiricality, it was the positivists' position on the last of those three that was largely definitive of positivism.[10]

The positivist position on the empirical. In the eighteenth century, British philosopher John Locke had been enormously impressed by Newton's accomplishments in science. Locke perceived Newton as having banned the nonempirical from science, and he thought that if restricting science to the purely empirical had proved to be the ultimate key to scientific knowledge (and who could doubt that?), then that restriction must be the key to other knowledge as well. That was the genesis of modern *empiricism*, the doctrine that all concepts, ideas and substantive knowledge available to human beings must ultimately rest solely on experience—in particular, on sensory experience or observation. The implication of this doctrine (forcefully advocated by David Hume) was that any alleged idea or belief that did not have empirical grounding was empty and literally meaningless.

This empiricism was welcomed by some of the leaders of the French Enlightenment, who were pushing toward a rejection of traditional authorities, including the church. The new empiricism, with the rising authority of science apparently behind it, gave them a powerful weapon in their battles with the church since much of church doctrine did not seem to be grounded on purely physical, sensory observation, reproducible experimentation and so on. What this sort of empiricism amounted to was of course an attempt to reduce all knowledge to scientific knowledge, all truths to empirical, scientific truths and all methods of knowing to empirical, scientific methods.

Although it fell out of favor to some extent during the romantic era of the early nineteenth century, a reductionistic empiricism was resuscitated in the twentieth century by the positivists. Their particular version of empiricism was built around the verifiability criterion of meaning. According to that criterion no statement is even meaningful unless either it is in principle possible to empirically verify it (or at least to test it) or else it is "analytic."[11] (An analytic statement is, roughly, a statement that is true just in virtue of the terms involved. For instance, *all bachelors are unmarried* and *2 + 2 = 4* are often considered analytic. Analytic statements generally express conceptual truths.) On this view it isn't that principles which are neither empirically testable nor analytic are merely unscientific or irrational but rather that they say absolutely nothing about the world at all, that they are literally meaningless. Positivists typically went even one step further and claimed that specific terms, including scientific terms, could not be legitimately used unless they could be defined strictly and completely in terms of sensory observation.

In any case, if the verifiability criterion of meaning was correct, any legitimate science would *have* to be empirical. And so would everything else that was not nonsense.

The positivist position on rationality. Positivists were leaders in the attempt to subsume the structure of science under logic.[12] But the early twentieth-century formal logic could deal completely adequately with only a restricted range of types of arguments and principles. Thus to make science fit into the formal logic model, all of the principles and inferences crucial to science had to be shown to fit into that restricted range. Consequently there was a great deal of work trying to specify the logical structure of, for instance, statements of the laws of nature using only resources for which formal logic was adequate.

But the characteristic positivist tendencies came out most clearly in the positivists' work concerning confirmation. As noted earlier one cannot prove some general theory or hypothesis true simply on the basis of specific observational instances. But if theories cannot be *proven* true, at least some theories are clearly more rationally believable than others in the light of available empirical evidence. The positivists tried to make that intuition formally rigorous and quantitative by showing that relative degrees of confirmation on the basis of empirical evidence conformed to some sort of logic, even if not exactly deductive logic. The most promising candidate was probability theory (specifying the probability of a theory's being true on the basis of a given body of evidence), and positivists expended considerable energy trying to determine exactly how particular positive instances conferred particular degrees of probability on the theories or hypotheses they were instances of.[13]

The positivist position on objectivity. Few have been willing to go as far as positivists in trying to keep science free of any possible subjective tinge. Virtually no one has been willing to go further, if indeed one could figure out how to do so.

The high-risk areas for subjective intrusion are theory invention and the smuggling into science of one's favorite metaphysical or religious or philosophical presuppositions. With respect to the latter, positivists claimed that most metaphysics, philosophy and religion were literal nonsense, and they tried to keep them out of science by constructing requirements for confirmation that such principles could not meet.[14]

With respect to the former, the positivists tended to be quite suspicious of theories—especially very general theories (since the generality made them extend far beyond actual observation) and theories that dealt with unobservable entities (atoms, electrons and so forth), since meaningfulness and observation were supposed to be linked. There was thus a strong antirealist tendency to positivism.[15] (Antirealists deny that science can or should produce genuine knowledge of unobservable entities or processes.)

Implications of Positivism

Perhaps the primary implication of positivism was an enormous epistemological reduction. According to the verifiability criterion of meaning, all knowledge (and indeed all legitimate human thought) had to be based on sensory observation. Science of course is the human discipline that deals most explicitly and thoroughly with the observable, and many saw it as the most spectacularly successful epistemological enterprise ever. It was but a short step from there to the conclusion that all real human knowledge was scientific knowledge. What science did not know or could not know was beyond the range of real knowing.

But if (as positivists thought) science knows only the empirical and what follows from it, and if science is the only human access to knowledge, then human knowledge is restricted to what is physical or material. There will be no religious knowledge and no ethical knowledge—at least for humans.

If one adds to that a high view of science—that the competence of science is in principle unlimited, that science can lead us to all truth[16]—then if all science can know is the material, the material is all the truth there is. Matter and the material forces that drive it will be the extent of reality.

The Decline of Positivism

Were positivism or something like it correct, the situation would be indeed bleak for religious believers and metaphysicians, two favorite targets of the positivists. But it became increasingly clear that the positivist outlook was bankrupt as a philosophy of science and ultimately incoherent as well.[17]

First, modern scientists have generally (not unanimously) been *realists;* that is, they have seen themselves as pursuing theoretical truth and trying to find out what the *sub*structure and *hidden* mechanisms of the world really are. Thus positivist antirealism is simply not true to scientific practice.

Scientists and others have also traditionally believed that science tries to provide explanations. Explanations, however, generally involve appeal to the characteristics and activity of various substructures and entities. For instance, we explain the shrinkage of balloons in terms of gas-molecule leakage. We explain the stability of some compounds in terms of valence electrons. We explain why you have your mother's nose in terms of genes. But the strict positivist cannot appeal to any of those explanatory entities since none are directly observable; they are theoretical entities. The positivist is confined to merely noting regularities in the shrinkage of balloons. If asked why they exhibit shrinkage regularities, the positivist must say basically that that's just the way it is. Some positivists have been driven so far as to deny that science has anything to do with explanations. It merely describes, they say. But to take that route is to strip science of one of its most distinguishing features—its theoretical and explanatory power.

The positivists' projects concerning rationality have not fared much better. The attempts to construct an inductive logic of confirmation failed without exception to be adequate to many real scientific tasks, although they did result in significant advances in probability theory itself.[18] Attempts to reduce natural-law statements to formal logic fared little better.

Their most serious failure, however, involved their foundational empiricist principle, the verifiability criterion of meaning. The principle fails in at least three distinct ways. First, it fails as a description of what is considered meaningful scientifically. Some basic principles essential to science are not empirically testable. For example, we cannot establish by experiment that nature is uniform. And that principle is not obviously analytic either. But such uniformity is a presupposition without which scientific tests themselves would be pointless. Second, the verifiability principle fails when applied to other sorts of specific examples. For instance, moral truths are not matters for empirical tests. We cannot *empirically* test the wrongness and sinfulness of murder, but to claim—as some positivists did—that such moral principles are cognitively empty is outrageous both philosophically and morally. Finally, the verifiability criterion of meaning is self-destroying. Is the verifiability criterion of meaning *itself* empirically testable? Clearly not. It is not an empirical principle at all but is a philosophical claim about meaning and the connection of meaning to empirical matters. And although some positivists attempted to claim that it was analytic, that did not seem at all plausible. But if the criterion itself is neither empirically testable nor analytic, then either it is itself meaningless (in which case we need not bother further about it) or else meaningfulness does not depend on empirical testability and analyticity, in which case the verifiability criterion is false (and we need not bother further about it).[19]

Thus positivism denies the legitimacy of the theoretical side of science (stripping it of explanatory power and rendering most scientists confused about what they are doing), causes problems for essential presuppositions of science, employs a defective theory of meaning and fails in its attempts to subsume all aspects of science under formal logic. Its one redeeming quality seems to be that it also destroys itself. But that particular positive achievement will hardly be a source of comfort to its advocates.

Oddly enough, positivism in one form or another is still influential in some disciplines, for instance, in some places in the social sciences and (of all places) in theology. There are also reportedly still two positivists among professional philosophers.

The Decline of the Traditional View
Although positivism was the most influential version of the traditional view of science and although the traditional view went into a decline not too long after the collapse of positivism, one could still retain the traditional outline without positivism.

There were, however, problems there too. For one thing, to the extent that the traditional and positivist projects overlapped, failures of positivism carried over as difficulties for the traditional view as well. Further, the equating of explanation and prediction did not seem quite right. If one knew the correct, purely empirical regularities, one could predict various things but might have no explanation for those events at all, just as ancient astronomers could predict eclipses but did not know why eclipses occurred. Thus prediction and explanation must differ in more than just whether the derivation is before or after the fact. It also follows that explanation cannot be simple deduction from empirical law since the ancients could deduce the times of eclipses from empirical laws but did not know what the real explanation or the real causes were. Besides problems of that sort, there was the perennial problem of trying to construct a logic—or even just an adequate theory—of how specific instances confirmed general theories and to what degree. There simply were no successful confirmation theories. Obviously philosophy of science had to look in new directions.

Popper and Falsification

Among early critics of positivism none has had as lasting an influence as Karl Popper (1902-1994).[20] Popper did not see metaphysical, philosophical and other nonempirical principles as being simply meaningless, and thus rejected the Verifiability Criterion of Meaning that constituted the very heart of positivism. But if these types of propositions could in principle be meaningful, that raised a *demarcation* question: exactly what constituted the criterion for distinguishing what was genuinely scientific from what was not?

As noted earlier, various positivists had attempted to construct a logic of confirmation. The basic idea, as usually construed, was that verified implications of a theory (correct predictions of or positive instances of the theory) conferred some degree of rational support onto the theory. Attempts to turn that intuition into a formal logic had failed, and Popper thought that (for a number of related reasons) all such attempts had to fail. First, and in most general terms, the whole idea of inferring the truth of some principle from the truth of its logical implications was, as Popper noted, "not completely impeccable from a logical point of view." (Any such inference commits the well-known logical fallacy of *affirming the consequent*.) Indeed, Popper continued, "[A] statement can never be finally established by establishing some of its consequences."[21] For one thing, any genuine scientific theory would have multiple consequences and would make multiple predictions. Thus even if those predictions that had been checked were correct, it always left open the possibility of future discovery that other implications were false.[22] And trying to get around this difficulty by checking *all* the relevant implications would, said Popper, be "clearly an impossible task."[23]

But there was a deeper problem. If particular empirical consequences (data, instances, predictions, etc.) could confer confirmation on a more general theory, that meant that there had to be some sort of "logical flow" from those particulars back to the theory. There had to be some logically legitimate move from the particular to the general—some logically legitimate mode of *induction*. But Popper argued that one could never logically legitimately infer theory from data[24] and that more generally "there is no such thing as induction."[25]

But even if the *truth* of a theory could not be established empirically, could we not legitimately accept some theories as *probable* on the basis of successful predictions, positive instances and other relevant pieces of empirical data? Not as Popper saw it. Popper viewed all genuine scientific theories and all natural laws as universal and general, applying to the whole cosmos and to potentially infinitely many possible instances. That infinity would create some mathematical problems. If we do one experiment covering one of the infinite possible instances, checking one of the infinite possible predictions, what percentage of the potential predictions of the theory in question have we verified? Essentially zero. Thus says Popper,

> One [could] ascribe to the hypothesis a certain probability . . . on the basis of an estimate of the ratio of all the tests passed by it to all the tests which have not yet been attempted. . . . [T]his estimate can, as it happens, be computed with precision, and the result is always that the probability is zero.[26]

In fact, that is true for any general theory "relative to [any] finite conjunction of singular statements"[27]—in other words, *no amount* of positive empirical data can ever raise the probability of a scientific theory above zero.[28]

So for Popper, theories are never verified or even verifiable.[29] We "can never give positive reasons which justify the belief that a theory is true."[30] In fact, "Our science . . . can never claim to have attained truth, or even a substitute for it, such as probability."[31] If science was to maintain its claim to be *rational*, it evidently had to give up any dreams of confirming theories.

But even if scientific theories could not be confirmed by empirical data, it looked as though scientific theories could still be *falsified* by empirical data. After all, it was logically legitimate to argue that if a theory generated an incorrect prediction, then the theory must be mistaken.[32] Popper concluded that falsification was the only approach left to science that was both data-based and logically rigorous. How then should science proceed? As Popper saw it, scientists should propose empirically testable, falsifiable theories, then test them as stringently as possible. Scientific progress would then consist not in developing theories that were increasingly, powerfully confirmed, but in systematic elimination of mistaken—falsified—theories. Popper described this as the method of "conjectures and refutations" (which was also the title of one of his books).

This, then, was Popper's answer to the question of what distinguished science from nonscience. A theory, hypothesis or other claim might be meaningful and important, but it was genuinely *scientific* only if it was empirically falsifiable or testable—that is, only if data could at least in principle contradict it and show it to be false. The core of Popper's demarcation criterion was that something was scientific only if it was genuinely at risk in the face of possible empirical data.

Popularizations of Popper often give the impression that Popper merely added to the standard view of science a slight new wrinkle consisting of the explicit criterion that theories only qualify as legitimately scientific if they are in principle empirically falsifiable.[33] But Popper's actual views were more revolutionary than popularly realized.

Since Popper equated the legitimately scientific with the empirically falsifiable, it followed instantly that if empirical data were legitimately scientific, then they too had to be falsifiable—an implication that Popper himself pointed out. Statements of empirical data had to be falsifiable and vulnerable to rejection by scientists. Scientific theories were supposed to be kept or rejected on the basis of empirical data—that was a key part of what it meant for science to be empirical. But then on what basis did one accept or reject empirical data themselves? Popper's answer was that an element of *human choice* entered science here:

> From a logical point of view, the testing of a theory depends upon basic statements whose acceptance or rejection, in its turn, depends upon our *decisions*. Thus it is *decisions* which settle the fate of theories.[34]

That of course represents a departure from earlier views with respect to the nature both of empirical data and of science. But Popper had less fear of human decision than did many others. For instance, he described his own falsifiability criterion as "a *proposal for an agreement or convention*" [his emphasis], described the methodological rules of science as conventions and remarked that his proposals arose out of his own "value judgements and predilections."[35]

Popper also rejected the standard picture of science as resting firmly upon an empirical bedrock. The picture Popper preferred was of a building standing on piles driven deep into a swamp (his example). The piles would never reach down to absolute solid bedrock, but if there were *enough* piles driven deep *enough* into the swamp, the building would be stable *enough* for intended purposes.[36]

As should be evident Popper's views incorporated some substantial, although sometimes subtle, departures both from positivism and from other standard views generally. Those departures—and the scope of their implications—are very frequently missed by those considering themselves to be Popperian falsificationists.

What are we to make of falsificationism? Is it correct? Both Popper's own version and the more familiar, popular versions of falsificationism face a variety of difficulties, of which I shall mention four.

First, Popper's own version in its rejection of the idea that any scientific theories are ever confirmed is certainly at odds with the views of the majority of practicing scientists, who believe that many scientific theories are indeed well confirmed.

Second, science is increasingly seen as inextricably interlinked with a number of nonempirical factors, including worldviews, philosophical presuppositions and the like. The range and depth of that interlinking is disputed, but to the extent that there is any at all, any attempt to distinguish science from other things strictly in terms of pure empirical falsifiability may face problems. That is perhaps a more serious problem for popular versions of falsificationism than for Popper who, recall, embedded human choice in science even at the level of the empirical.

Third, even ignoring possible "interlinking" issues, falsificationism of the popular sort simply does not seem to work quite right. Consider this claim: somewhere, sometime, the universe has contained or will contain a perfectly cubical piece of gold weighing exactly ninety thousand and three kilograms. Intuitively there is nothing inherently *unscientific* about that claim—it is not nonempirical, is not metaphysical, does not contain hidden reference to some unobservable realm, or anything of that sort. It is even consistent with all known scientific laws and may even be *true*. But even if it is false, there is no way to show by *any* amount of empirical observational evidence that the statement is false. Thus popular versions of falsificationism are simply not correct.[37] (Popper himself recognized that such "existential" statements were not empirically falsifiable and concluded that despite appearances all such statements were actually *metaphysical* statements.[38])

Fourth, and worse yet for popular falsificationist views, as we will see a bit later, *no* logically consistent scientific theory can ever be conclusively shown to be false.

Whatever its difficulties, Popperian falsificationism represented a significant challenge to some aspects of the traditional view, even though that fact frequently went unrecognized. But the most serious challenge to traditional conceptions of science came in part from a different direction.[39] The challenge was so serious that some believe that the traditional picture of science is now only a historical curiosity. The challenge has deep roots. To trace its development we must once more go back a few centuries to the eighteenth century and Immanuel Kant.

3

Philosophy of Science in the 1960s & 1970s
Kuhn & Beyond

From at least the seventeenth century it has been recognized that some of the principles necessary to science are not empirically provable. In fact, the British empiricist David Hume argued convincingly that the uniformity principle could not be proven by any means available to humans.[1] But since science required that principle, its use required justification in order to preserve the general rationality of science itself.

One influential response to that problem came from Immanuel Kant.[2] Accepting Hume's conclusions concerning the logical and empirical unprovability of uniformity, Kant argued that various categories and principles of thought were built into the very structure of our minds and into the very operation of our perception. Any experiences we had were organized according to these categories and principles before we even had conscious access to them. Thus if we knew what these categories and structures were, we would know something about any future experience we could ever have, since it would always be organized in the way dictated by the structure of our minds and the operation of our perceptions.

Imagine a person watching a 19-inch black-and-white TV. If he understands the TV's working, he can know that he will never see a 25-inch picture on the screen and that he will never see a red rose on the screen regardless of how long he waits and regardless of who is broadcasting what from where. The set simply cannot deliver such pictures. Moreover, any picture he does see will be two-dimensional and will be grainy if examined close-up because the set imposes those characteristics on any picture it shows. Similarly, on Kant's view, if we know the structures of the mind and perception, know what constraints they dictate and what characteristics they impose, we can know some things about any experience we can ever have.

After much argumentation Kant concluded that the principle that nature is uniform is one of the principles by which all our experiences are organized. Thus although we cannot prove the truth of the uniformity principle, we can know that no experience we can ever have will violate that principle since conformity to that principle will be imposed on any experiences we can ever have. We can, then, use the principle with perfect confidence, knowing that it will never be empirically undermined.

That was an elegant solution to the problem of justifying the use of the uniformity principle, and it applied also to principles of causation and other former trouble spots as well. But it came with a substantial price attached. Since our experiences were formed, shaped and even partially constituted by these structures within us, and since our only access to the world outside ourselves was via experience, all we could study directly and all we could really know about scientifically were our own experiences, our own perceptions. Since our experiences were in part the results of subjective alterations that took place even before we were or could be conscious of those experiences, we had no reason at all to think that they corresponded to ultimate reality. Kant, in fact, thought that it could be shown that whatever reality in itself was like, it *could not* be like our experiences of it. Thus science gained the legitimate use of the principles it had to have but lost the external world it was supposed to be studying. This view of science—science as the studying of and organizing of nature *as we perceive it* rather than of nature as it is in itself—is a type of *idealism*. As should be evident, this type of idealism is antirealist.

Kantian idealism enjoyed varying degrees of popularity, but that type of thinking received a major boost from developments within physics around the first quarter of the twentieth century. The two major developments were relativity and quantum mechanics. Although the philosophical consequences of those developments are still disputed, a few basic implications are fairly clear. Relativity implies that various observational measurements one makes are in part consequences of the state of the observer, and quantum mechanics is taken to imply deep connections between the observer and the observed. The connections are so deep that one respected contemporary physicist has suggested that it may be that the universe "had to adapt itself from its earliest days to the future requirements of life and mind," that our universe is a "participatory universe" and that through our observation we are somehow tied into a "partnership in the foundation of the universe" (an extreme version of the currently much-discussed "anthropic principle").[3] Although not explicitly Kantian the most influential movement within philosophy of science in the 1960s and 1970s was built around the general idea that various mental facets of human beings affected not only what a person actually and truly perceived but even to some extent the reality that was being perceived. And the major figure at the beginning of that movement was a person trained in theoretical physics, Thomas Kuhn.

Kuhnian (or "Postempiricist") Philosophy of Science
The positivist conception admitted humans into the processes of science only grudgingly and admitted humanness into science not at all if it could be helped.

But the misanthropism of positivism was becoming increasingly out of step with the resurgence of romanticism (or at least some sort of humanism) that characterized the 1960s. It was probably only a matter of time before someone developed a philosophy of science that swept hard objectivity, thorough empiricality and rigid rationality to the fringes of science and established humans at the very center of science. That era began in 1962 with the publication of Kuhn's *The Structure of Scientific Revolutions*.[4]

The single most important and basic component in the Kuhnian conception of science is the notion of a *paradigm*. A paradigm is, roughly, a standard of scientific achievement in terms of which scientific work is conducted and evaluated.

Let us look briefly at a historical example, the Newtonian paradigm. After Newton, one was simply not taken seriously as a physicist or, in some cases, even as a scientist if one did not do science *as Newton had done it*. For instance, Newton's work had been characterized by symbolic generalizations—his mathematical equations. Newton's work had also presupposed some metaphysical commitments—for example, that matter in deterministic motion was the fundamental and revealing feature of nature. And Newton had placed high value on accuracy of prediction, measurability of results and observability of subject matter in his experimental philosophy. Just exactly how all of those various components were to work together could be seen in his exemplars, actual examples of scientific problem solving displayed within Newton's work itself. If you had pretensions of being a scientist, your work had to display those characteristics and had to be consistent with Newton's generalizations.

Those four constituents—symbolic generalizations, metaphysical commitments, values and exemplars—are nearly definitive of paradigms. A paradigm is those four constituents (plus perhaps others) integrated into a unitary scientific outlook, or a "disciplinary matrix."[5] The paradigm, then, contained not only theoretical postulates but also presuppositions about the world that those postulates were to fit, about how they ought to fit that world, about the proper procedures for trying to make them fit and criteria for judging when such attempts were or were not successful.

According to Kuhn the history of science is the history of the careers of various paradigms, some involving several disciplines, some involving only small groups of specialists. In fact Kuhn argued that science had to be *defined* in terms of paradigms and that in the absence of paradigms there was no such thing as science.[6] But what struck him most was his perception that scientists did not behave toward paradigms as the traditional view would lead one to expect. In particular, scientists seemed to simply *assume* that a particular paradigm embodied the correct approach to nature[7] and seemed not to be particularly concerned with either verifying its correctness (it was *already* taken as being correct) or with trying to falsify it (if it is correct, trying to show it as incorrect seems pointless).

What then are scientists generally trying to do if the focus is not on confirming or falsifying theories? Kuhn's answer is that scientists are generally trying to figure out how to account for various phenomena and observations in the terms and categories dictated by the paradigm. A paradigm is typically proposed in light of some limited collection of scientific experience and within some limited area. The main concern of scientists most of the time is to push the paradigm into new scientific territory, seeing how far it can be made to extend, clearing up ambiguities in the paradigm or, as Kuhn terms this sort of activity, articulating the paradigm.[8]

According to Kuhn there are only two other types of routine scientific activity. First, a paradigm may imply that some specific type of data is particularly important and revealing. The scientific community will attempt to obtain that particular information. Second, the paradigm will have some predictive implications that have not yet been checked. There will generally be some effort at running such checks. But these types of activity are in general secondary concerns, and they are subsidiary to paradigm articulation.[9]

The periods during which a discipline or scientific community accepts or shares the same paradigm Kuhn calls periods of *normal science*.[10] Normal science is thus investigation bound by a shared paradigm, and it consists largely of puzzle solving, solving puzzles concerning how to apply the paradigm to new phenomena.[11] During periods of normal science the shared paradigm serves to define the relevant discipline or scientific community (those who do not accept the paradigm are labeled pseudoscientists or worse), to define what are legitimate scientific problems, to define what are acceptable solutions to problems, to guide research and to suggest new lines of research.

Paradigms also generate expectations concerning the results of new experiments or research, and here the fun sometimes begins. Sometimes actual observational results are contrary to what the paradigm leads one to expect. A result that is contrary to the paradigm-generated expectation is an *anomaly*.[12] Normal science turns up anomalies surprisingly frequently.

What, according to Kuhn, do scientists do when an anomaly surfaces? Sometimes they do not even seem to notice the anomaly, and sometimes when they do, they simply ignore it.[13] Usually, however, there is some attempt to show that the apparent anomaly is not really an anomaly after all, that someone simply made a mistake somewhere. Maybe there was a miscalculation, or maybe someone dropped part of his lunch into the beaker. Sometimes such attempts are successful. But sometimes they are not, and the anomaly apparently stands as a fact contrary to the paradigm. What do scientists do then? Sometimes nothing. Despite its being contrary to the paradigm, scientists may simply view it as being an *unimportant* violation of the paradigm.

But occasionally an anomaly resists usually successful methods of solution for such a long time that scientists grow uneasy. Or an anomaly may involve something so central to the paradigm that it cannot be ignored. Sometimes the sheer number of anomalies becomes alarming.[14] In these cases (and perhaps others) anomalies begin to get serious attention, and the discipline may enter what Kuhn terms a *crisis state*.[15]

During a crisis state a discipline basically suffers a breakdown. Its confidence in the previously shared paradigm disappears, and its unanimity behind that paradigm is replaced by a flurry of new alternative paradigms and a fragmentation of loyalty. Ad hoc proposals abound, and the discipline begins squabbling over its philosophical foundations and presuppositions. The situation is obviously dire indeed. The discipline mobilizes against such a threat and turns its major resources on the problem.[16]

Crisis situations get resolved in one of three ways.[17] First, the troublesome anomaly may yield to a solution within the bounds of the old paradigm. If that occurs, then the discipline regroups and returns to normal. Second, no solution in terms of the old paradigm may be found, but none of the new proposed solutions may be acceptable either. In that case the discipline may decide that the resources for dealing adequately with the crisis may not be available, and it may return to the original paradigm (knowing that the paradigm may already be mortally wounded) and leave the problem for some future generation when there will be perhaps more money, better equipment, more powerful mathematics or even better scientists available.

The third type of crisis resolution is a scientific revolution. A scientific revolution, on Kuhn's definition, is the replacement of an old, dented paradigm with a new one, around which the discipline then organizes itself and within which scientific investigation is conducted. The discipline then enters a new period of normal science. This alternation of periods of normal science with episodes of crisis sometimes punctuated with revolution is Kuhn's picture of the history of science.

Although there are no rules for when a revolution will take place, two conditions are necessary. First, the old paradigm must be in trouble. Second, there must be an acceptable alternative available. Given the key role that Kuhn sees for a paradigm, to abandon one paradigm without putting another in its place is to abandon science itself.[18]

It will be recognized that at several important points Kuhn departs from the traditional view of science. For one thing, the inclusion within science of both metaphysical and value principles violates the letter both of the traditional view and of the positivist view. For another, the apparently cavalier attitude toward anomalies is seriously at odds with a literal reading of the hypothetico-deductive method.

But those apparent departures may not be so radical as at first appears. We have seen that science cannot do without metaphysical principles (uniformity, for instance). And the values that Kuhn builds into paradigms are neither arbitrary nor subversive of science. They include accuracy of prediction, simplicity, fruitfulness, measurability, what features of a phenomenon it is important to explain and so forth.

The matter of attitude toward anomalies might seem more serious. If science is to let nature have the final say regarding theories, it will hardly do to blithely ignore nature when what nature says is at odds with our paradigm-generated expectations. But maybe the ignoring is not always irresponsible. There have been historical cases where a paradigm seemed at odds with nature but subsequently turned out not to be, at least on the count in question. Had scientists given up the paradigm at the first hint of trouble, scientific progress would have been held up until scientists came back to the very paradigm they had abandoned too quickly. In other cases, even though a paradigm was ultimately overturned, much was learned from the research carried out under that paradigm, and the refusal of scientists to dump the paradigm too quickly did not result in wasted time and effort. In many cases the tenacity with which science holds onto paradigms challenged by anomalies has been to the benefit of science.

Thus on a casual look at the Kuhnian philosophy it might seem that, although there are differences from earlier views, those differences merely constitute needed modifications to the traditional view, leaving the general traditional outlook intact.

Looking Deeper

Such a view would be a serious misconception. As one pushes more deeply into the Kuhnian picture, it becomes increasingly apparent that there are deep departures from the traditional picture. Built into the very foundation of the Kuhnian view is a human-dependent wholism that leads to enormous differences with the traditional view.

By *wholism* here I mean that view that the component parts meld into such a unity that even the nature of the parts themselves is affected by that unity. The nature of the whole is in some sense determinative of the nature of the parts themselves. Kuhn's scientific wholism is founded on a wholistic theory of perception and a wholistic (or coherentist) theory of meaning.

Some psychologists have recently argued that one's expectations, mindset, conceptual framework and in some cases specific beliefs have some effect on one's perception, on what one sees. If that is true, then perception is an active process and not (as traditionally held) the passive process of having things outside ourselves imprint objective information on our minds through the neutral medium of our senses. There is, on this view, much more of our person involved in perception than just isolated, inactive sense organs. (Compare Kant here.)

Kuhn accepts a view of this sort and holds that among the factors shaping perception are the paradigms we accept.[19]

This has two important consequences for science. First, by influencing perception, paradigms will sometimes prevent one from even recognizing anomalies.[20] That is why, according to Kuhn, scientists sometimes do not even see anomalies that might otherwise cause difficulties for their paradigms. Clearly the empirical, objective nature of science is weakened if paradigms not only modify perception but sometimes prevent one from seeing counterinstances to one's theories.

Second, according to Kuhn, adherents to different paradigms would sometimes not be able to see quite the same things.[21] Their differing paradigms would make different contributions to their perceptions, making those perceptions in some degree different. But if that is true, then observation would not be a purely neutral process and the neutrality of observation, cited earlier as objectifying science, would be lost. There would no longer be any perfectly neutral database by reference to which adherents of differing paradigms could objectively settle their differences. Paradigms would be partially constitutive of the very *seeing* that the database was built on.

Kuhn also argues that paradigms are involved in the meanings that we attach to particular terms.[22] If that is true, then people with different paradigms will use some of the same terms to mean at least subtly different things. Thus even if they use all the same terms and sentences, they will not be saying quite the same things. There will be to some degree a failure to communicate, a talking past each other.[23] If so, scientific language is no longer neutral, and the loss of that neutrality in communication will at least partially destroy the *communal* objectivity of science. If people cannot even fully understand each other's scientific pronouncements, how can they keep each other honest? With the effects of paradigms on perception and meaning, the way is open for the subjectivity of particular scientific communities to be woven deeply into science.

But even more radical results are yet to come. On older views it was presumed that there was a single correct method and a single correct set of evaluative procedures. But according to Kuhn, method and evaluation are themselves part of paradigms. They may vary from paradigm to paradigm and may thus change when paradigms are switched during revolutions.[24] Furthermore, there is no *ultimate* arbiter among such principles, so none is "righter" than another. They are merely different, one paradigm stipulating one set, another paradigm stipulating another, although the one paradigm might be in some sense more successful than another.[25] That being the case, an ineradicable relativism may be embedded in science.

These points together imply an additional consequential result, also recognized and accepted by Kuhn. Since holders of different paradigms cannot even make all the same observations (perception), and since they will have a hard time communicating to each other what they do observe (meaning), holders of different paradigms will have a hard time comparing their paradigms in order to settle their disputes. And since their respective evaluative judgments will be directed by their paradigms, which may contain different evaluative criteria (relativism), they could not objectively resolve their differences even if they could manage the comparison.

There is yet more. Kuhn suggests that in some sense one's paradigms are partially constitutive of one's world. It is not just that with different paradigms we see and mean differently (although he means at least that), but that in some sense that Kuhn has difficulty defining, the *worlds* to which our paradigms address themselves differ.[26]

Although getting Kuhn's view clear is complicated by his ambiguous use of "world" and "nature"[27] what Kuhn apparently has in mind is this: the only access we have to any world is through perception, and perception is paradigm-colored. On Kuhn's view, without something like a paradigm there could be no perception.[28] Since perception essentially involves our paradigms, and since perception is the *only* access we have to "the world," it follows that we have no access independent of a paradigm to any independent reality.[29] *Our* world, the world of our perception and thus the only world we have access to, is "jointly determined by nature and a paradigm."[30] There really is something out there (the "environment") that is independent of us and that does not change when our paradigms change,[31] but we cannot get at it except via perception, which means we cannot get at it free of a paradigm. (The Kantian flavor is evident here.) Therefore, when our paradigms change, *our* "world" changes as well.[32] Thus, says Kuhn, after a revolution scientists are working in a different world.

Since we can never get at any *independent* environment, on Kuhn's view, we cannot always appeal to it as referee for scientific disputes. Even in principle we can only get at the mixed worlds that are "jointly determined" by our paradigm and that environment, so some disputes involving different paradigms will of necessity be irresolvable by appeal to the empirical for the simple reason that there will be no *unique* world to which we all have access. The different worlds the opponents will have access to will be partly constituted by the very paradigms at issue, meaning that not only will there not always be neutral data that can be extracted from those worlds, but some of the very data extracted will beg the question at issue.

All of these consequences concerning meaning, perception, communication, the nonneutrality of data, and "worlds" are clustered around what Kuhn terms the "incommensurability" of paradigms.[33]

What does Kuhn mean by "incommensurable"? He is sometimes accused of meaning that competing paradigms cannot even be compared with each other, but he actually means something weaker since he explicitly says that some kinds of comparison *are* possible.[34] But there is, on his view, no complete comparative procedure that is normative for all paradigms. Paradigms divide reality up in different ways, with different metaphysical assumptions, different methodological principles and different values. The components of one paradigm (and of its world) generally do not stand in any simple matching relationship to the components of a different paradigm (and its world). Each has a structure and flavor which are not completely reducible to the resources of the other. In fact, Kuhn suggests that it is probably impossible for a single mind to hold two competing paradigms before itself and do a point-by-point comparison.[35] A mind in the grip of one paradigm apparently cannot quite grasp all of another.

All of these differences have serious consequences for the dynamics of scientific revolution. When a revolution takes place and one undergoes a paradigm shift, perception, meaning, observational data, even the world within which one works all change, according to Kuhn.[36]

On what basis does one decide to undergo such a monumental change? It cannot be by *simple* comparison of competing paradigms, if that cannot be done. Nor can the basis for the switch be just observational data if observation is paradigm shaped and if the different paradigms determine different worlds to be observed.

Thus according to Kuhn there is no complete, *logical* procedure for paradigm shifts.[37] Certain sorts of comparisons are possible, but the change, when it occurs, is like a Gestalt switch,[38] or, as Kuhn sometimes says, a "conversion."[39] Thus the key events in the progression of science—revolutions—are discontinuous and without any strict determinative logic. Not only is there no determinative logic for paradigm choices, but the values that partially constitute paradigms play a fundamental and unavoidable role in almost all scientific decisions.[40] Applications of values are not strictly rule governed. Competent and rational people can disagree over *how* accurate a theory must be, over *how* important explaining some particular phenomena might be, or even over which of two values *should* take precedence in cases of conflict. Thus there will almost always be a range of positions with respect to paradigm choices, theory choices or other scientific disputes, *all* of which will be rational. The character of those decisions as, in part, *value-decisions* will guarantee that latitude.[41]

Of course, in construing scientific decisions as possibly rational despite the absence of strict logical rules for making such decisions, Kuhn is rejecting the traditional equating of rationality with some sort of determinative logical procedure.[42] And in arguing that we have no paradigm-independent access to some ultimate reality and that paradigm choices are in part value choices made by scientists, Kuhn is moving the ultimate court of appeal concerning correct pictures of reality away from the world itself and toward the informed consensus of scientists.[43]

Finally, since our paradigms partially constitute our worlds, worlds will be as variable and subjective (communally) as paradigms are. Since there is no complete and stable and independent external reality to which we have access, there is no particular point in talking about truth in science (except of a relative sort).[44]

Still, Kuhn does admit that there is something stubborn out there when he speaks of scientists having to "beat nature into line" to get it to fit a paradigm.[45] That phrase is revealing. On the traditional view, nature beat our theories into line. That was the hallmark of its objectivity. On Kuhn's view, scientists try to beat nature into line with their already-accepted paradigms, which they have accepted on some non-logical value-shaped basis. That reversal is the hallmark of its (communal) subjectivity.

But whatever is out there does not allow itself to be shaped in just any direction. At some points a paradigm ceases to work very well and a crisis results; that is, nature strikes back. In fact, Kuhn sees it as one of the virtues of normal science that it does so often lead to anomaly and crisis. In its attempts to reduce all reality to the reigning paradigm, normal science is a particularly effective way of guaranteeing that spots of trouble between the paradigm and the otherwise inaccessible environment will force themselves into our attention, thus eventually precipitating revolution to a more successful paradigm.[46] It is in revolution to more successful paradigms that the progress of science lies.[47]

But the Kuhnian movement has placed humans and human subjectivity (in the form of values of the community of scientists) firmly in the center of science. It has emphasized that science is a decidedly human pursuit. Science is seen as no more ruggedly and rigidly objective and logical than the humans who do it.

Although Kuhn's views represent a substantial departure from previous views, there are still similarities with the past. In fact, older views could not be *just* mistakes and confusions.[48] Although we could not get at it independently of a paradigm, there was still some independent reality out there that did not admit of being bent indefinitely into any configuration we happened to choose. Although perception was paradigm shaped, empirical data (in particular, those representing anomalies) played a key role in precipitating crises. And although there were no complete, specifiable logical rules governing paradigm changes, science was still seen as a rational pursuit.[49]

But in the years since Kuhn first published his views, a number of more radical repudiations of traditional conceptions of science have emerged. Some have maintained a basically Kuhnian structure but have built various non-Kuhnian components into that structure. Some have retained basic Kuhnian themes but have pushed them far beyond the point to which Kuhn himself was willing to pursue them. Other views have arisen from quite non-Kuhnian foundations. Following are brief discussions of a number of such alternatives.

Radical Kuhnianism

While Kuhn placed human value judgements near the heart of science, the values selected were those important to the inner workings and concerns of science itself—empirical adequacy, simplicity, consistency and the like.[50] But some have taken such values to be inadequate. For instance, it is obvious that science can only go as far as human conceptual and intellectual resources can take it. Those are all we have. Some claim that women, minorities and other traditionally "voiceless" groups have unique conceptual resources, different from those of the groups that dominate theory construction (generally Euro-white males).[51] Some who hold this position argue that science should seek to cultivate those alternative conceptual resources.

In fact, some maintain that the ultimate success of science might *depend* upon such alternative conceptual resources. Nature might confront us with phenomena that could only be properly understood in terms of such resources. If the only voices possessing necessary insights are ignored or silenced, scientific failure would be guaranteed.[52] For instance, some argue that a science in the unconscious grip of a traditional outlook can see and seek order in nature in terms only of dominance hierarchies and power (natural *laws*) and is thus blind to other possible types of order to which, for example, women would be more attuned.[53] Some types of order might be visible only to empathy, not to rigid analysis. Such order might involve, for instance, a flowing of nonreproduceable complexities—an order that rigorous, analytical (reductionistic) approaches simply could not get a grip on.[54]

Thus some believe that science should in its own interest incorporate sensitivity to unique perspectives of marginalized social groups. Although advanced as an *epistemic* value, the flavor of this value is significantly different than that of any on Kuhn's list. Some commentators abandon even the idea that the relevant values should be *epistemic* (or even that there *are* epistemic values). As some contemporary critics of science see it, a science can claim legitimacy (if at all) only to the extent that it furthers a "human-friendly" agenda. On this view scientific theories must be evaluated and accepted or rejected not only on familiar truth-seeking bases such as empirical adequacy but also according to such criteria as promoting social inclusiveness, diffusion of social and political power, fostering social diversity, meeting human needs and antireductionism.[55] The difference between these values and Kuhnian values—let alone traditional evaluative criteria—is stark indeed.

In some views the hints of idealism and subjectivism in Kuhn have become more explicit, resulting in claims that "what counts as the real world depends upon our values," that "we must have criteria of rational acceptability to even have an empirical world" and that without certain "'cognitive values' . . . we have no real world and no 'facts.'"[56]

Although Kuhn thought that there were no complete and determinative rules of rationality, he did maintain the rational character of science. But others have gone beyond Kuhn here too. For instance, it has been claimed that "allegiance to the new ideas will have to be brought about by means other than arguments. It will have to be brought about *by irrational means* such as propaganda, emotion, ad hoc hypotheses, and appeal to prejudices of all kinds."[57] Furthermore, views that are essential parts of science "exist today only because reason was overruled at some time in their past."[58] Thus, if science insisted on proceeding by only rational means (whether logically structured or not), it would quickly dissolve, and we are consequently advised to "let [our] inclinations go against reason *in any circumstances,* for science may profit from it."[59]

Kuhn believed that scientific "truth" was in part sociologically determined by factors within the scientific community. Many have adopted that position and have explicitly embraced the relativism and historicism they see it implying. For instance, it has recently been argued that scientific knowledge is whatever scientists of a particular era accept, and scientific truth is whatever scientists know in that sense. Thus the beliefs of scientists determine what truth is, and truth will change along with their beliefs. It is frequently objected that the mere fact the scientific community agrees on something does not mean that is the way things really are, or that scientists' belief does not determine *real* truth. In response to that objection we are told that *that* sense of Truth "has no relevance for the evaluation of theories since theories provide the only access we have to reality."[60]

Others have expanded the sociologically relevant domain to include the larger society beyond the scientific community and have drastically expanded the scope of sociocultural factors. On Kuhn's view, while human factors played a significant, unavoidable and indeed constitutive role in science, an external reality (the "environment") also played an important role, and the picture that science built was not simply an arbitrary human fabrication. But according to some more radical views science is embedded in a wider social context, and even its most definitive functions—theory selection, data interpretation, theoretical concept formation and the like—interlock into wider sociocultural structures and are partially determined by them. Sometimes, more radically yet, even the "partially" gets dropped, generating the position that science is a wholly sociological phenomenon and that even what science takes to be *facts* are simply *social constructions.*[61] As some see it, social forces (whether involving just scientists or the wider community as well) are the *only* constraints on scientific theory construction, evaluation and decisions, which would otherwise be completely "free and unconstrained."[62] Some claim that the very *existence* of theoretical objects such as quarks consists *only* in the agreement of scientists arrived at through "negotiations" of a special type that is characteristic of science.

Some have claimed that objectivity itself is "a social phenomenon"—in particular, that "institutionalized belief . . . is what objectivity is."[63] But in one very straightforward sense a science that is completely socioculturally created is a science devoid of objectivity and neutrality, having various social preconceptions, philosophical outlooks and agendas in its very bones. Indeed, those would *be* its bones.[64]

Postmodern Pictures of Science
There is another (partially overlapping) cluster of more deeply radical

pictures of science, generally identified as *postmodern* conceptions of science. Although some postmodern thinkers take Kuhn as one spring-board for their views[65] and endorse various of the above positions, the perception which most postmodernists have of science has both a dif-ferent source and a vastly more negative flavor than those above.

Postmodernism is too diverse to be given a simple definition. But postmodernists share a nonnegotiable hostility to what they take to be the defining views of *modernity*—the conceptual and cultural struc-tures associated with the scientific and social revolutions of the six-teenth through eighteenth centuries.[66] Those views include the ideas that there is an independent and objective reality, that there is thus only one objective Truth (one correct, global, all-encompassing story or *metanarrative* about reality), that each of us humans is an indepen-dent, autonomous center of reason capable under the right conditions of grasping that Truth, that in doing science we can meet those condi-tions, and that science thus has a privileged perspective through which we can acquire objective and neutral knowledge of the Truth of reality. Such views, postmodernists claim, are not only viciously mis-guided, but they have carried us inexorably to the brink of social, eco-logical, conceptual and spiritual disaster. And that, as they see it, is not mere unfortunate coincidence. Rather the very foundational con-ceptions of modernity itself drive the destruction.

But although united in opposition to modernism, postmodernists exhibit unanimity on little else. That makes it extremely difficult to characterize any substance of postmodernism, but the following cov-ers what I take to be its core.

Our conceptions and perceptions of "reality" are ultimately struc-tures encompassed by *language*. We can only *understand* in terms of language, so any "world" that we can understand, and any under-standing we have of it, must be language-structured. Therefore, any reality we are in touch with must be clothed in or structured by—or even constituted by—language.[67] But language is, of course, a socio-cultural artifact, and it necessarily has built into it the defining fea-tures—dominance hierarchies, power structures, prejudices and so on—of the culture that creates and is created by it. Thus any reality we know—and perhaps any reality there is—is socially constructed and fundamentally reflects nothing but the structure of the constructing culture.[68]

Kuhn argued that we cannot get outside our own paradigm, and many postmoderns have taken that type of position as axiomatic—that not only is our language-laced reality constructed from a specific perspective but that we cannot get outside that perspective. We are always inescapably inside our own conceptual space.[69]

> What we cannot do is to rise above all human communities, actual and possible. We cannot find a skyhook which lifts us out of mere coherence—mere agreement—to something like "correspondence with reality as it is in itself."[70]

Furthermore, no culture, institution, group or individual has any special, preferable, privileged perspective on "real" reality. Thus among the competing conceptual constructions, the competing pictures of reality, the competing metanarratives, none are any closer to some alleged *truth* than are any others. (A number of postmodernists take the underdetermination of theory by data to establish this equality of perspectives.)[71]

Not only can we not get to any "correct" general picture of history and reality, there may not even *be* any such all-encompassing truth. Indeed, the influential postmodernist Jean-Francois Lyotard simply defines postmodernism as "incredulity toward metanarratives." The traditional Western insistence that there is one "right" perspective (and that Western society has it) has inspired a history of violent cultural and intellectual imperialism against other perspectives. Indeed, that insistence itself very nearly *constitutes* such violence.

Science of course lies near the heart of the worldview of modernism. On the postmodern view a fundamental problem with modern science (and with the worldview of modernism generally) is that the ineliminability of perspective, the equal legitimacy of all perspectives, the absence of objective truth and the like are not only unrecognized but even explicitly denied. Modern science, with its pretensions of being "rational," "objective" and "empirical," proudly boasts that *it* is the exception, that *it* really does have a privileged vantage point, that *its* edicts really are true—as if they were not also mere constructions by humans. But not only does science not have any *privileged* perspective (there simply *isn't* any such), according to some postmodernists it has no *relevant* perspective at all.[72] If reality is ultimately a function of *language,* then the only relevant methods of approaching it would be those appropriate to approaching a *text* or a *narrative,* and science's analytic, linear, reductionistic thinking is far off target.

So as many postmodernists see it, the picture science produces of reality (or reality itself) is human invention. And since that picture takes its shape from the prejudices of the inventors who themselves typically represent a socially dominant group, that very shape has an *inherent* potential as a vehicle for perpetuating the sociopolitical dominance of that group.[73] The *real* subtext of science is simply the repressive perpetuation of social power and privilege.[74]

What then becomes of the traditional characteristics of science seen from a general postmodernist perspective? Well, the empirical is a free human construction, driven by and constrained only by impinging social forces. Objectivity, in the sense of anything human-free, has been banished. Social effects run so deep that even such allegedly rationally pure disciplines as logic and mathematics are subject to "the contamination of the social."[75] In fact, the idea of scientific neutrality is *itself* just a socially enforced, socially manufactured modern myth. Rationality turns out to be merely a confining characteristic favored by and claimed by the culturally dominant group currently in control of science.[76] And the realism crucial to the conceptions of science held by most scientists and many philosophers of science becomes merely an "aesthetic."[77]

As one would expect, postmodernists tend to hold science in (to use a wonderful seventeenth century phrase) "vile esteem." After all, the very theories of science embody the confusions and repressive stances of modern culture. Given such pollution, could anything like science be salvaged? For some that would require a revolutionary change in science, and given science's cultural embeddedness that could only happen in conjunction with revolutionary social changes—which many postmodernists demand in any case. For others, were science to submit itself to the "service of progressive interests" (as defined by postmodernism), then it could become legitimate.[78]

But from a postmodern perspective, whatever one's position on the possible correctability of science, one should keep in mind the depth of confusion that science as it is now conceived embodies. For instance, when science claims to turn up some fact, we should remember that

> [a] fact is . . . a neuter past participle in our Roman parent language [and that we should not be] worshipful of a past participle.[79]

Second, when constructing our worldviews we should insist on freedom *from* science, recognizing that

> there is no obligation upon anyone framing a view of the world to take account of what twentieth-century science has to say. . . . In [some] contexts, to listen too closely to scientists may be simply to stifle the imagination.[80]

Is there then anything to be said *for* science from a postmodern perspective? For some, very little:

> The only sense in which science is exemplary is that it is a model of human solidarity.[81]

So in keeping with the postmodern primacy of social values the only positive thing to be said for science is that scientists have found ways to reach agreement—not that the content of their particular agreements have any genuine significance or special worth.[82]

Reception: Postmodern and Radical Kuhnianism

Postmodern views (at least in full-blown form) have not been accepted by most professional philosophers of science or by scientists themselves. That is not to say that many philosophers of science and many scientists do not share some of the concerns that partially motivate postmodern thinkers. For instance, many share some of the social aims of postmodernists but do not take such concerns—important as they may be in their own right—as of any *epistemological* significance to science itself. Many admit that underdetermination *is* a worrisome fact of scientific life. And it *is not* always clear whether or how we can get outside our own standpoints in order to evaluate the theoretical, conceptual landscape—or even how important that might or might not be. Science *is* inescapably embedded in a wider social context, and that fact *has* affected the course and content of science historically. Our conceptual resources *are* at least partially shaped by our perspectives, and our human science obviously *cannot* go beyond our human conceptual resources. And science *has* been involved in destruction and repression, not merely in terms of the (mis)uses to which politicians have put science, but sometimes more substantively—in terms of racist biological theories advanced by reputable scientists for example,[83] or in terms of theories that reduce humans to mere mechanisms. But despite acceptance of those premises, most scientists see postmodern conclusions about science as merely faddish and empty posturing by people with little if any clue concerning what real science is even about and who grossly misunderstand the very science they purport to criticize.[84]

Most philosophers of science have not been much more sympathetic. For instance, postmodern views have been criticized as being self-defeating in exactly the same way as was positivism. Postmodernism seems to say in effect that *all* views are irreparably trapped in their own perspectives and thus cannot rightfully critique other perspectives, all of which are equally legitimate, while simultaneously insisting on immunity to application of those principles to itself, implicitly claiming that the postmodern perspective is correct, that it is *the* right approach to the issues and that consequently it is superior to all other perspectives.

Postmodern views have also been attacked for the claim that reality is a social or linguistic construct, and various postmodernists have been fervently invited to empirically test the theory that gravity is merely a social or linguistic construct by flinging themselves off tall buildings. That is related to the conviction that one prominent feature of science is that in some sense it *works* and that it works on nature's terms—not just on ours or on those of our society or on those of our language. Critics claim that it is not clear that the more extreme views that reality is ultimately social or linguistic can even begin to accommodate that simple fact—a fact that has a bit more substance than merely that of a past participle.

The more radical extension of Kuhnian positions have also not achieved much long-term success.[85] What motivates many such views is a conviction that truth cannot have a decisive bearing on theoretical science. The truth is held to be unavailable to us. After all, if we cannot even *perceive* without a paradigm (as Kuhn argued), if we have no neutral, non-human-tinged access to external reality, then we can never set bare reality alongside our theories and step back and compare reality and our theories to see if indeed they do match, that is, to see if indeed our theories are true.

And if truth is unavailable, then we must settle for what we can get—for example, the consensus of the scientific community as defining "truth" and "knowledge." If we cannot get beyond whatever reality we perceptually engage, then we must settle for that as a definition of what counts as the real world. If we cannot escape past our social imprinting, which will inevitably tinge all we do and think, then society itself must be behind (or above) scientific knowledge. It must define objectivity.

It is of course true we do not have somewhere a text that contains all scientific truth, one to which we can directly compare our theories to see whether we are on the right track. The Nobel Prize committee does not have an answer book against which to check proposed theories. But it hardly follows that truth in the usual sense is irrelevant to science. There may well be criteria by which we can judge theories, and we may have philosophical or other reasons for thinking that theories that satisfy them tend more likely to be true than theories that do not. Adopting such criteria as values within science would thus allow truth to have (at least in principle) some bearing on theory choice.

But if science *can* move over time toward theoretical truth (whether it ultimately gets there or not), then a (or the) motivation for the more radical views will collapse. And if science *can* move toward truth and if such movement is a goal (thus a value) of science, then some constraints and procedures will be more appropriate and rational in seeking that goal than others. It is the view of some contemporary philosophers of science that there indeed are such truth-tending values, and we shall look at some of them later. In any case, the pronounced subjectivism, relativism and irrationalism of the more radical views have not won the day.

There are also other difficulties with views at this end of the scale. Some of them incorporate a theory of perception (like Kuhn's but more extreme) that is not at all obviously true. Although prior beliefs might well affect expectations, interest and direction of attention, it is not clear that two people with different paradigms, backgrounds, theories and so on, looking at, say, the number displayed on a meter *see* different things. What they make of what they see and the significance they grant it may well be different, but that is another issue. Surely scientists working out of different theoretical frameworks sometimes see *exactly* the same thing, their arguments being about proper *interpretation* of what they both see. Thus the more thoroughly one pushes the idea that "all observation is theory laden," the less plausible it becomes.

The conception of meaning often presupposed in radical views (like Kuhn's but more extreme) has also come under attack. People with sharp differences in theory or outlook or paradigms might well attach different associations to the same term and might disagree over the term's range of application, but that is not to say they *mean* something different by it, that different concepts are involved. Were that the case, it would be hard to account for *any* communication between scientists with different theoretical frameworks. But there obviously is such communication. Here again, the further one pushes this position, the less plausible it becomes.

Perhaps the most vehement objections to radical views have been directed toward their irrationalism. There may be little agreement on exactly what rationality means and even disagreements over whether specific cases are cases of rationality, but it seems perfectly eccentric to deny rationality to science. What might be meant by the term *rational* if we deny application of it to science?[86]

Difficulties with Kuhnian Views

One could reject the foregoing radical and postmodern positions and still maintain a conception of science like Kuhn's, but a number of Kuhn's own positions have attracted criticisms as well, and Kuhn's explicit views do not have the influence now that they did in the 1960s.[87] What are some of the difficulties?

Two that I will simply mention and not discuss are (1) that the notion of "paradigm" was never satisfactorily defined[88] (which would seem to be important given its centrality to Kuhn's system) and (2) that it is not at all clear that Kuhn had interpreted the history of science correctly (and such an interpretation was the foundation for much of his system).[89]

Kuhn has also been criticized for the doctrines of perception and meaning incorporated by his position.[90] When the positions in question are pushed to their extremes, unacceptable results ensue. Although Kuhn does not appear to follow either position to the extremes discussed earlier, he does tend to follow them further than many current philosophers of science believe to be warranted.

Kuhn has also been frequently criticized over his claims concerning incommensurability.[91] Some of those criticisms have rested on a misreading of Kuhn. But Kuhnian incommensurability depends of course on the paradigm-bound nature of observation and meaning, and to the extent to which Kuhn may have overemphasized the force and range of such effects, his claims concerning incommensurability will be too broad as well.

Finally, the tacit idealism and the rejection of the relevance of truth (in any nonrelative sense) to science have become increasingly out of key with contemporary philosophy of science. We will explore that issue more fully in the next chapter.

Kuhn has, however, made important contributions to the study of science. One of the most important has been in the area of scientific rationality. Kuhn seems right in his contention that theory adjudication and settling of scientific disputes are not (in principle) the rote, mechanical process envisioned by the positivists but that scientific decisions often involve applications of values (in Kuhn's sense). Consequently scientific decisions often exhibit some of the characteristics of value-decisions, in which there are generally no completely explicit, completely determinative *rules* governing acceptance of particular values, weighing of values or application of values to specific cases.[92]

Following Kuhn, philosophers of science have also become more aware of some of the dynamic aspects of science and their role in scientific rationality. They have become convinced that the very character of science can change over time as its values change and as what is taken to be "scientific method" changes. Kuhn has helped show the importance of scientific tenacity, of scientists at least for a time staying with a theory beset with anomalies in place of the rudderless open-mindedness of being blown about by every wind of data, which was advocated by earlier views. He has made explicit the importance within science of metaphysical principles. And philosophers have become increasingly convinced that Kuhn was right in thinking that the history and practice of science can provide important clues and constraints on theorizing about science.

Also following Kuhn, philosophers of science have begun to pay more attention to the human side of science, to see it as in some ways essential to science. The fact that science is done by subjective humans is no longer seen as the regrettable factor it was once taken to be. Science is increasingly taken to be an undeniably human pursuit.[93]

But though there has been a movement away from many of Kuhn's views, a simple return to some earlier position would not do; the difficulties of those positions are well-known. Kuhn has in that respect provided a needed corrective to the rigidity, formality and autonomy of earlier conceptions, and those lessons are not to be forgotten.

The precise direction to take is not exactly clear, but it has become increasingly apparent where the direction should be sought. In some sense the positivists and the later followers of Kuhn and other radicals were at opposite ends of one scale. Both seemed to think that rationality, objectivity and empiricality were all-or-nothing propositions. The positivists opted for the "all" end with all three. As much as possible everything had to conform to a rigid logic, subjective factors had to be isolated and detoxified, and everything had to rest on the empirical (empiricism). At the other end the major episodes in science (revolutions) were nonrational. Subjectivity entered even into perception. And the empirical sometimes could not so much as be seen; if it was, it could often be safely ignored. Both extreme sides accepted the all-or-nothing assumption, disagreeing only on which end to jump to.

But it is not at all clear that the choice is between "nothing goes" or "anything goes." Contemporary philosophy of science has been searching for some middle ground where reason, observation and objectivity have an appropriate place but where the human factor is at least that—a factor.

4

The Contemporary Situation
A Brief Introduction

Contemporary philosophy of science has tried to incorporate the lessons of the Kuhnian approach without losing the insights of earlier periods. But there are a number of ways of doing that. As with any discipline there are unresolved problems and disagreements. Rather than attempt to survey all such disagreements and all of the currently competing positions, we will look briefly at some views within the emerging mainstream in philosophy of science, admitting that some will disagree. We will start with one contemporary way of viewing the three characteristics we have been following to this point. Then in chapter five we will look with greater depth at specific issues.

Empirical Data

As we have seen, the positivists went to the extreme of empiricism and gave such a high role to the empirical that *any* piece of recalcitrant data was supposed in principle to prove fatal to any theory it contravened. On the other hand Kuhnian paradigms were relatively immune to contrary data. At least contrary data did not bring about the instant collapse of the paradigm.

Something is right and something wrong about both positions. Empirical data do not cut quite the swath through theories that traditional views suggest, nor do they bounce harmlessly off the armor of all theories as some postempiricist views would have it. Science does respond, sometimes rapidly and decisively, to empirical data, although in other cases it strongly resists the apparent push of some bits of data. Is there any overall pattern to these varying responses?

One current answer is that we must distinguish at least two levels of theory. One level (variously called "maxi-theories" or "research programmes" or "research traditions")[1] comprises the broad, conceptual frameworks within which the day-to-day activity of science takes place. The other level consists of the more detailed, specific theories that are attempts to deal with particular phenomena within the constraints imposed by the maxi-theories. Within this lower level, alternative "mini-theories" compete for any given area or set of phenomena, all of them falling within the bounds of the maxi-theory, which, being more general and programmatic, does not settle the issue in favor of any one of the specific competitors. For example, chemists typically agree that material substances are to be analyzed in terms of their constituent components, and they agree on the physical configurations of those components, the various bonds between them and the external forces acting on them. They typically agree further on the nature and number of the types of components (standard elements), the general constraints on configurations (molecular geometries), the types and nature of the possible bonds, and the types and nature of other external forces. But earlier in this century there were extended debates over the physical basis of heredity. Different theories were proposed, all of them within the above framework, but all were ultimately rejected on empirical grounds except one—the double helix theory. But even had all the proposed *specific* theories been rejected on empirical grounds, the *general* framework within which the proper specific theory was sought would not have been in jeopardy.

The key thing to see is that empirical evidence bears on these different levels in different ways. The maxi-theories are relatively difficult to move, and it takes an enormous amount of empirical pressure to shift them. Maxi-theories usually encompass many specific theories covering a broad range of phenomena. And if many of the specific theories are highly confirmed, the maxi-theory under which they operate is also strongly supported and therefore has sizable empirical inertia. Thus there is usually good reason for reluctance to abandon it and good reason to hope that apparently contrary data may eventually be shown to have interpretations acceptable within the bounds of the maxi-theory. But there are no rigid rules for determining when that hope is no longer rational.

On the other hand, the specific mini-theories are much more subject to the immediate effects of empirical data. They are, again, simply attempts to solve problems within the broader framework set by the maxi-theories. If one such attempt does not work, perhaps another will. Science often has little historical investment in any particular one of them, and if the data tend to show that one of them is inadequate, the loss to science is minimal. No other part of science need be affected. But a maxi-theory is a synthesizing, simplifying and unifying factor within science, bringing numerous mini-theories into a system of shared fundamental principles. So abandonment of a maxi-theory would turn a previously conceptually unified area of science into a disorganized collection of isolated, independent, unrelated mini-theories without common conceptual anchors.

Thus the relative (although not complete) immunity of theory from obstreperous data as found in the Kuhnian system seems right with respect to the large-scale framework theories of science. The relative fragility of theories in the face of contrary data as envisioned by the traditional views seems right with respect to specific, smaller-scale theories within that larger framework. Thus some theories are rejected straightforwardly on the basis of contrary data, and some theories persist in the face of such data. But the theories in those respective categories tend to operate on different scales and play different roles within science.

On this view, then, science is still significantly empirical, although especially with larger-scale theories the influence of the empirical is tempered, ensuring that there be some theoretical stability to science, and that the clear historical continuity of science (which earlier views had to deny at various points) can be accounted for.[2]

Objectivity

On the traditional view, objectivity was guaranteed. Anything other than the empirical was not allowed to affect theory evaluation, and observation was considered neutral. On the Kuhnian conception, however, other factors played a role in judgments concerning theories, and perception was paradigm determined.

It is now generally conceded that things other than just the empirical bear on theory evaluation and theory choice. Judgments are generally made against the canvas of one's *background beliefs and commitments*—other theories, beliefs, values or commitments one has that bear on the acceptability of theory, data or their relationship.[3] Often such judgments are subject to nonscientific influences as well. The question of what beliefs and commitments *ought* to influence judgments in science is unsettled, but few hold out for the older position that only the observable ought to carry weight. Few, however, are willing to allow that just anything whatever should influence scientific decisions.

The empirical does of course play an important role in contemporary conceptions of science, but that would not produce objectivity were perception not neutral. Some investigators currently take positions between extremist subjectivity and positivist absolute neutrality.[4] They argue that background beliefs influence *some* perceptions but that *not all* background beliefs have such influence and that *not all* perceptions are so influenced. For instance, some illusions we continue to see in illusory fashion even when we know that they are illusory and even when we know why we see them as we do. Thus the knowledge we have in those cases seems to leave our perception unaffected. And no matter how passionately we hold some contrary theory, we cannot succeed in perceiving more than one moon in the sky at a time. (Kuhn's own position is moderate on this issue.)

Further, the history of science contains many occasions when significant theoretical advances were made by scientists looking at old data in new ways or in terms of new concepts (e.g., Copernicus and Galileo). But it was still the old observational data they were reinterpreting. If there were not at least a core of neutrality in the relevant observations, it is difficult to see how those same observations could lend themselves to use in multiple, substantially different theories.

Thus no matter how much some background beliefs might affect some perceptions, there remains a substantial core of perceptions that are neutral, shared with other humans and perfectly capable of giving contrary theories indigestion. And if theories cannot insulate themselves from such contrary observations, and if those observations are shared by other observers as well, there will be a basis for objectivity in science. Science will have at least some objective touchstones.

In fact, there will probably be many such touchstones. One notable feature of science has been its tendency toward consensus among scientists. If there were no objective constraints on theorizing, that consensus would demand some special explanation. Kuhn and some others appeal in part to sociological factors to explain it: a certain faction gains control of the schools, textbooks and journals, and simply reads any dissidents out of the discipline, thus giving a unanimity—at least in appearance. Current tendency, however, is toward the view that the *core* of neutral, common perception provides objective constraints to keep the community of scientists going in the same general direction and that scientific consensus is not simply a sociological artifact, even though sociological factors may play a more or less significant role in particular cases.

Rationality

According to the positivists the rationality of science was to be in terms of rigid, logical procedures for each aspect of science. Kuhn, however, saw the major events in science as proceeding in a manner more closely resembling value-decisions than formal logical arguments. Some of the radicals saw science as either nonrational or irrational, sometimes explaining the history and practice of science in psychological or sociological terms. Current positions tend toward the Kuhnian view that science is indeed (usually) rational but that rationality is not formally and rigidly rule governed.

In some broad sense rationality—scientific or otherwise—involves acting and choosing in ways that seem likely to accomplish our overall goals.[5] One major goal of science is understanding or explaining various parts of nature. (Prediction and control of nature are major goals, but understanding is, I think, primary.) Understanding is linked to truth. We do not really understand a phenomenon if our explanation of it bears no relation to reality. Thus getting closer to theoretical truths must be an underlying goal of science.

It is indeed hard to believe that science is not rational and that scientists are not often rational in accepting one theory and rejecting another. Yet one can no more specify explicit sets of *rules* for determining precisely when acceptance or rejection of a theory is rational than one can set rules for determining exactly when a novel becomes implausible or exactly when someone has strayed from the bounds of common sense. Think of jury trials. The objective is to determine whether certain things are "beyond reasonable doubt." Although some cases are disputed judgment calls, many such decisions are unproblematic. But there is no complete set of rules for making such decisions. If there were, juries would be superfluous. The case is similar in science. Those working in a field generally acquire a feel for what is rational, and often we have to rely on their educated judgment on the matter. This does not, however, mean that there are no independent, nonsubjective constraints, that scientists just plain do not make mistakes, or that any scientist's decisions are beyond external criticism. The core objectivity of science still makes such criticism and its communal base both relevant and important.

It is even possible for the entire scientific community to get off the rails. Although the scientific community usually exhibits rationality collectively, we cannot simply *define* whatever they do as rational. Sometimes the entire scientific community goes in a particular direction for highly suspect reasons or as a result of sociological pushes. Thus while rationality usually characterizes the actual directions of a discipline or scientific community, we need to recognize that even scientific communities are made up of humans, all of whom can go astray in unison. Their unanimity does not automatically render the straying rational.

What might justify thinking that there is something rational about a scientist's feel for when things are or are not going scientifically right? One possible justification is the same kind of faith we have in our perception. Perception produces beliefs within us—about cars, trees and other objects—which we normally cannot help accepting and which are typically *rationally* acceptable. Similar factors are at work in our formal thought. We cannot help but accept that $2 + 2 = 4$, and we take that acceptance to be *rational* and take nonacceptance to be irrational. In our common sense we accept innumerable beliefs needed to get through any given day and could not refuse to accept them if we tried. We take that acceptance to be *rational* and put those who do not accept them under observation. In each of these types of cases we take beliefs that arise normally and involuntarily out of our make-up and situation to be rational and their rejection to be irrational and a sign of something being amiss.[6] We are generally unable either to explicate fully the process by which the beliefs arise or to construct complete sets of rules by which we might in fact be making the relevant judgments, although there are partial lists of relevant rules.

Science is often called organized common sense. If scientists are led partially in their judgments by a perhaps heightened version of the familiar common-sense processes (their "feel" for the discipline) and if our common sense is as reliable and rational as we routinely take it to be, then scientific rationality may have no special difficulties, being just the organized extension of that more general rationality. But why should we think that there is any connection between *truth* and the beliefs that arise involuntarily in us? We will discuss one Christian approach to that question later.

Of course, there must be more to the story than what has been said to this point. Many philosophers of science have followed Kuhn in his insistence that values play a major role in scientific decisions and consequently in the nature of scientific rationality.[7] In fact, it is on Kuhn's view the ineradicable presence of a value component to scientific decision-making that ensures that such decisions cannot be reduced to some set of rules.[8]

There is currently a lack of clarity concerning what all the values in science are. Kuhn's list includes the following: a good theory should be empirically *accurate, consistent* (both internally and with other accepted scientific theories), *broad in scope* (and extendable to new phenomena and into new domains), *simple* (in the sense of bringing together what are otherwise apparently different and unrelated phenomena) and *fruitful* (in pointing to new phenomena and uncovering new relationships among previously known phenomena). And as he admits, there are others.[9]

Kuhn believes that these five have been more or less universal among scientists in all paradigms.[10] But even that universality does not make for unanimous decisions among scientists. For one thing, other values often play roles as well. But more important, since these values are not rigorously precise (*exactly* what does "broad in scope" mean, for instance?), not everyone will apply them identically.[11] Further, they sometimes point in conflicting directions. For instance, one theory might be broader but less simple than its major competitor. In that case a scientist must decide which of the conflicting values is to be weighted more heavily. And of course, intuitions may conflict over exactly which value outranks another. Empirical accuracy is, however, generally given pride of place in the long run, but often *not* in the short run.

In any case, the values that figure into science do not seem reducible to some set of rules. That does not, however, make the values employed or their application arbitrary, nor does it make the scientific decisions they figure into either irrational or free of rational constraints. Some values will serve the goals of science more effectively than others, and we can perhaps learn what those proper values are from the track record that various values have compiled in actual scientific practice and history. If we take science as producing real knowledge about an objective reality, as philosophers of science increasingly do,[12] then finding where and how such knowledge has tended to be produced and what *epistemic* values figured into the production can perhaps help to justify rational acceptance of particular values.[13] Such a process will be substantially philosophical, and it will be partially circular since it will employ the accepted results of the application of various values in the evaluation of those very values. But that circularity might be virtuous rather than vicious. In any case, independent *philosophical* justification might be available for some values. Complete sets of automatic rules are not specifiable, and we must rely upon human judgment in many areas. But those features of the scientific case are consistent with the pattern of human rationality in other areas, as we would expect, given that science is, after all, a human pursuit. The overall perspective here is that scientific rationality is of a piece with human rationality in other areas.[14] The pattern of that rationality will, however, more closely resemble that of common sense or value-decisions than that exhibited in the strict logic cases that historically provided the accepted model for rationality.

Summing Up the Contemporary Situation

Pieces of observational data are extremely important. They can be objective, theory neutral and shared by all the members of a scientific community. They must sooner or later be dealt with in some hard-to-specify but rational manner—a manner involving not just logic but applications of value and value-decisions as well. But given that difficulty of specification, there is still room for disagreement among scientists over relative weights of values, over exactly when to deal with recalcitrant data, and over theory and evidence.

But such disagreements often take place within the context of broad background agreement concerning the major presuppositions of the discipline in question. This broad background of agreement is usually neither at issue nor at risk. It has a protected status similar to that Kuhn claimed for individual paradigms. These research-programmes or maxi-theories are strongly resistant (although not immune) to challenges, while the specific mini-theories that operate within their confines have a more tenuous hold on scientific allegiance. Thus objective empirical data have substantial and sometimes decisive influence on individual theories, but they have a more muted impact on the larger-scale structure of the scientific picture of reality. However, if the empirical assault is serious enough (and there are no rules for "serious enough"), even the more ponderous maxi-theories can be made to move. Thus objectivity, rationality and empiricality have been making a significant comeback over the past two decades or so.

But if there is a backing away from the radical end of the scale, don't many of the old problems resurface? Yes, they do, and much current work within philosophy of science is involved with reevaluating older issues in the light of Kuhn's lesson that humans are intrinsic to science and the subsidiary lesson that the actual history and practice of science can provide clues to philosophical puzzles concerning science.

One cluster of issues has especially come to the fore in philosophy of science. In chapter five we look at those issues and at the direction in which contemporary philosophy of science seems to be moving with respect to them.

5

The Competence
of Science
*What Can It
Tell Us?*

T*he realist-antirealist debate has been mentioned briefly in the*
preceding chapters. This debate is basically a dispute over what scientific theories actually tell us. The realist believes that in principle theories are to be taken literally to some degree, that to some degree they
provide us with actual descriptions of the underlying structure of
nature or with actual truth. The antirealist believes that theories cannot and do not tell us any such thing. Science may tell us much, but
the information it generates does not constitute revelation.

In this chapter we will explore the issue of what science can tell us.
We will discuss what theories are, their status with respect to conclusive proof or refutation, the outlines of the realist/antirealist dispute,
and the underlying dispute over and problems with empirical confirmation of theories.

Theories and Models

Preceding discussion has touched on scientific theories, but the term *theory* has not been explicitly defined. As with *science* there is no universally subscribed definition of *theory*, although most conceptions of what a theory is cluster together rather closely. For present purposes we will use the term *theory* to refer to a network of propositions, some of which involve theoretical concepts, which (ideally) provides a systematic, rigorous account of some portion of the natural realm.[1] A *theoretical* scientific concept we will take to be a concept that has application, if at all, to physical entities, processes or events not directly observable.

One relatively popular view is that a theory consists of a formal calculus (a set of equations), interpretation of the calculus (providing the meanings and the empirical significance of the symbols used in the equations) and a set of empirical laws (the empirical consequences deducible from the equations as interpreted). Competing with that view is one which stipulates that a theory is not complete without a conceptual model that allows us to intuitively visualize the entities, events and processes to which the other components of the theory refer.[2] This *visualization* is taken to be crucial since it is, on this second view, only through that visualization that we can in any sense be said to *understand* what the theory describes. That understanding usually involves being able to construe the unseen, theoretical matters in terms of things with which we are already familiar. It is a *reduction to the familiar.*

For example, consider the kinetic theory of gases. The theory involves a number of equations (Newtonian dynamics, for instance), some statements relating the components of those equations to empirical observables, and the empirical generalizations generated from those two constituents of the theory (classical empirical gas laws). On the second view of theories, the scientist must provide a way of visualizing what those equations and statements are about. In a gas case this is usually the billiard-ball model: we should think of a gas as being composed of tiny, hard, round particles, like miniature billiard balls, with lots of free space in between. These particles are in rapid motion, and they sometimes collide with each other and with the walls of the container. When they do, they bounce off and continue in motion, in obedience to Newtonian dynamics and just like miniature billiard balls. The collisions with the container walls account for pressure phenomena (relating the components of the equations with the empirical). Compress the container and there will be less space for the molecules to travel, hence more frequent collisions with the container walls, hence increased pressure (a classical empirical gas law). Thus the observed increase in pressure of a gas being compressed *is accounted for* by this visualization of a familiar process translated into an unobservably small scale, and the equations of collision and rebound behavior are supposed to account precisely for the measurable increase in pressure. (The same model and equations are also supposed to account for a variety of other gas phenomena.)

The two views of theory (one rejecting conceptual models, the other requiring them) also generate different positions concerning what theoretical terms mean. Those holding the first view argue that theoretical terms must be given any meaning they have in terms of the observations to which the theory connects them. As it turns out, none of the specific attempts to flesh out such a demand have worked satisfactorily. Those holding the second view argue that the conceptual model, the analogical visualization of the theoretical matters, can itself provide part of the meaning of the theoretical terms—a part that has wider resources than just the empirical matters directly tied to the theory. These attempts have shown much more promise than the former.

The two views also differ concerning if and how a theory provides an *account* of reality. Advocates of conceptual models argue that the model provides us with an understanding of the events the theory is about; after all, with proper visualization we can simply *see* how and why decrease in the volume of a gas results in increase in pressure. Those who reject the essential use of such models have in some cases with the positivists denied that explanations (if they are tied to models) have any place in science at all.

For present purposes, models will be taken as essential. Some of the reasons for that will emerge in subsequent discussion. For simplicity we will stay with the characterization of a theory as a network of propositions, some of which involve theoretical concepts, which (ideally) provides a systematic, rigorous account of some portion of the natural realm, with the implicit proviso that the explanatory accounts typically involve understanding through reduction to the familiar.

Why Theories Cannot Be Proven True

We have already seen that science does not provide any means of proving the truth of empirical generalizations. When we come to testing theoretical matters, the case is even more problematic. We test a theory by examining its *observational consequences*. When we want to test a theory about, say, exotic particles like pi mesons, we must have not only theoretical postulates about what pi mesons themselves are and do but also principles about how pi meson activity—which we cannot directly see—is translated into something we can see. Otherwise we might have the right pi meson postulates but think that they were wrong because we had mistaken observational expectations. The connections between purely theoretical matters and purely observational matters are usually called *correspondence rules* or *bridge principles*. If we had no principles telling us how events on the unobservable theoretical level affected events on the observable empirical level, we could make no empirical predictions on the basis of a theory, and we thus could not test the theory observationally at all.

But that raises a sticky problem. How do we arrive at the correct principles for bridging the gap between the unobservable and the observable? We cannot do it solely by observation, because the bridge principles deal with both observable *and* unobservable. And we cannot very well just make them up.

Theoretical principles are thus no more provable than empirical generalizations. Not only do we run into all the earlier problems (limited data, the possibility of future counterexamples, reliance on such principles as uniformity), but given the unobservability of the theoretical, testing cannot even be done without bridge principles; and trying to prove the correctness of particular bridge principles brings us right back to some of the original problems.

Here again we see the logical tentativeness of science. The data do not drive us inevitably to correct theories, and even if they did or even if we hit on the correct theory in some other way, we could not prove its correctness conclusively.

Why Theories Cannot Be Proven False

It is widely believed that even if we cannot prove the truth of particular theories, we can save some of the certainty of science because we can often prove the falsehood of some theories. That view, however, is mistaken.

Theories generally do not *by themselves* imply any empirical predictions at all. To deduce an observational consequence of a theory one has to take into account a number of additional factors. For instance, one must make some assumptions about the experimental equipment one is using. If the machinery does something other than what one believes, then the results of the experiment will probably be unexpected whether the theory being tested is right or not. Those assumptions are often unproblematic, but for a complicated apparatus one's beliefs about what it does will be based on other *scientific theories* one holds. For instance, what goes on in the interior of a cyclotron involves parts of electronics theories, particle theories or field theories, and so on. Thus experiments involving use of a cyclotron will normally include the assumption that those *background theories* concerning cyclotron operations and cyclotron results are correct. But as we know, theories are never conclusively proven correct. Those assumed theories are therefore still tentative even if they have been confirmed to a very high degree and even if we have great confidence in them.

Suppose that a test of a theory involves use of a cyclotron and that the results are contrary to the theory's prediction. The theory is not thereby proven wrong, because although something is wrong somewhere, the mistake might be in the background theories about which we have no absolute guarantee. There are other factors relevant here as well. But the upshot is that when a predicted result fails to materialize, the tested theory is not thereby conclusively proven to be mistaken since other things that were essential in the derivation of the prediction have not been conclusively proven to be right.

The Status of Theories: Realism and Antirealism

The fact that scientific theories can be neither conclusively proven nor conclusively disproven appears to some to have profound consequences. If the true theories cannot be proven true and the false theories cannot be proven false, how can science give us real *knowledge* about the world?

With simple inductive generalizations (e.g., that all water boils at 100°C) one merely projects observed patterns into unobserved regions of space and time; and although one cannot *prove* that generalization, the uniformity of nature at least makes the projecting plausible. It is, after all, the very same pattern that has actually been seen which is attributed to other parts of space and time.

But with theoretical, unobservable matters—such as electrons, genes, quarks and so forth—the situation is vastly different. No one has ever actually seen an electron. Evidence for electrons is indirect, often involving other theoretical matters as well. That evidence (pointer readings, cloud-chamber tracks and so on) is observable, but it is employed in support of nonobservable theoretical matters (electrons). The connection between the empirical base and theoretical conclusions is less straightforward than in the simple generalization case. In the electron case we are dealing with projections across levels—theoretical claims about *un*observables based on data about observables. How can we justify such cross-level projecting into a realm we neither have seen nor can see? How are we to justify belief in electrons, protons, genes, quarks and so on in a science that is supposed to be empirical?

The empirical seems to exert a much looser control over theory than many had thought and hoped. If there isn't any logic for inventing theories, if there isn't any absolute scientific proof, if there is no known logic of confirmation, if there isn't even any way of *rigorously* eliminating the most woefully false theories, can there be any justification for taking any theoretical pronouncements seriously? Other historical periods have confidently accepted theories that turned out to be wrong. Why think our favorite theories are exempt from that historical pattern? How *ought* we to take theoretical pronouncements?

A sharp dispute over the exact status of theories has existed for years. On one side are realists and on the other are antirealists. Let us look at their positions in more detail.

Antirealism

Antirealism comes in a variety of types.[3] For current discussion we will distinguish three categories, although the types in question are not necessarily mutually exclusive.

First are what we may call "ontological antirealisms." There are at least two distinct types within this category. One type denies that reality holds any hidden structures, entities or processes. It claims that the macro-world is the fundamental level of reality. The second type is a form of idealism claiming that, while subobservational entities and so forth may be real, we humans somehow produce them.

The second general category we will call "linguistic antirealism." Views in this category share the positions that theoretical terms, such as *electron,* do not refer to real things and that if theoretical statements are true at all, it is not in virtue of or with reference to hidden, unobservable matters.

Some advocates of this position, including many positivists, argue that terms and principles are legitimate only if they can be defined in words describing observations.[4] But if a theoretical term by definition just means something concerning observation, then it does not really refer to some unobserved but real thing, just as *average person* does not refer to some actual object, but is a shorthand way of talking about frequency of characteristics of larger groups. Similarly, on this view *electron* would not be a referring term, referring (or purporting to refer) to some very small but real entity, but would be a shorthand way of talking about observations of various sorts.

Other linguistic antirealists claim that theoretical terms are defined by the operations one employs to measure certain effects (*operationism*).[5] For instance, *charge* might be defined by the movement of a needle on a meter or the deflection of certain types of objects. In talking of charge, according to the operationist, we are not referring to some mysterious force that we fortunately know how to measure with the right instruments. Rather, it is the very measurement with those instruments that defines the term *charge.*

On both of these types of linguistic antirealism, theoretical statements may well be true, but what they are true *about* are not unobservables but either patterns in observations or patterns in observational measurements.

Some antirealists in this general category hold that theories are not even the sorts of things that can in principle be true. The terms *true* and *false* do not apply to theories. On this view, theories are simply abstract rules or instruments for calculating, making predictions and otherwise dealing with observational matters (hence, *instrumentalism*). Rules are neither true nor false; they rather are or are not appropriate, effective or adequate for some specific task. Similarly, according to instrumentalists, theories are either adequate or inadequate but not true or false—much less true about unobservables.

A third general category of antirealism may be called "epistemological antirealism." On this view, theoretical statements can indeed be either true or false, and theoretical terms can indeed refer, but there is little chance that our human theories are right and no way of ever finding out what the theoretical truth really is.[6] That, says this antirealist, is especially plausible in light of the facts that we can offer no proofs either way, that whatever evidence we might have can in principle be explained in innumerable ways, and that almost all historical scientific theories have been rejected. This type of antirealism amounts to a theoretical skepticism. Still, fiction though they be, theories are often useful for predicting and for devising technologies for the control of nature. So we can use these useful fictions *as if* they were true, but we should not make the mistake of confusing that usefulness with actual truth.

There are other types of antirealists, but they too have in common a refusal to accept literally construed theoretical beliefs as ultimately true. They also generally take *empirical adequacy* (yielding correct empirical predictions) as the basic criterion of theory acceptability.

Antirealisms have several positive features. For one thing, antirealists can avoid all the nasty epistemological questions concerning the justification of belief in unobservables (since they all reject such belief) and concerning theoretical confirmation. Since they do not claim to know what happens on some unobservable plane, they do not have to try to figure out how it is even possible to know such things. For another, antirealism fits quite nicely with the view of science as purely empirical, which prompts some scientists to say that all they do is observe and describe, and that if you do not like the results, take it up with nature.

But antirealism has difficulties too, and the drawbacks are serious enough to have turned philosophy of science in a realist direction over the last quarter century. Many of the difficulties have already been discussed in connection with positivism—for instance, lack of faithfulness to the realist tradition within the scientific community and the stripping of science of its explanatory power (in any ordinary sense), since explanation is often in terms of substructures not directly observable.

We have not yet discussed one other difficulty. If various theoretical principles are not on the right track, it is difficult to account for the success science has had in predicting entirely new phenomena, phenomena often *observationally unrelated* to either the phenomena for which the theory was originally proposed or to anything else previously known.[7]

For instance, in the early 1800s physicists were embroiled in debate over whether the wave or the particle theory of light was correct. Simeon Poisson, a particle advocate, pointed out that the then-current version of the wave theory had the startling and totally unanticipated implication that a point source of light shone onto a circular object should produce a round shadow with a bright spot in its center. That predicted result was so far removed from any reasonable expectation arising out of any known observational phenomena that Poisson advanced it as an obvious refutation of the wave theory. However, the prediction turned out *correct,* which gave a major boost to wave theories of light.

In such cases there is nothing whatever in the old *observational* data that would even hint at the new phenomena. Yet the theory predicts them, and when someone checks, there they are. If the whole notion of the theoretical does not involve doing something right—if theories cannot get beyond the mere observed level of reality—those sorts of cases involve the most wild of coincidences. Coincidence, however, has always been a scientifically suspect notion. For that and the other reasons mentioned, contemporary philosophy of science has shown a strong realist tendency.

Realism

Realism is the view that theories can be true and accurate descriptions of objective reality, that theoretical terms can actually refer to real entities having (at least some of) the properties we think they do, that we can know that certain theories are true and can know that the entities and processes they purport to refer to are indeed real, and that such descriptions and knowledge are at least aims of science. There are, however, varying degrees of realism, varying views of the sort of truth theoretical truths are and various views concerning when realist claims become legitimate.

Let us define first what we may call "hard" realism. A hard realist holds that our theories are or can be completely and literally true, that the statements of a correct theory are true in exactly the way we humans understand them, and that all the substantive theoretical terms they contain refer to real, existent entities having the properties the theory stipulates in exactly the way we think they do.

As can be readily seen this hard realism involves some enormous and sweeping claims. It has been attacked on a variety of grounds. For instance, given the fate of the theories of virtually every historical period, why think that *this* time we have gotten it *exactly* right? And if subjective and human factors affect at least some of our thinking, perceiving and theorizing, why think that the way we happen to (or have to) theorize about reality *could* be *exactly* the way things are—especially in the light of some of the startling results of twentieth-century quantum mechanics and relativity? And keep in mind too that data underdetermine theories; that is, they do not prove or establish any specific theories, and any body of data can be explained in any number of alternative theoretical ways. Even if we hit on the exactly correct theory, even if our concepts exactly fit nature, how would we ever be justified in *claiming* that to be the case? How could we ever get confirmation that this was the case?

In light of such considerations, most of those who have wanted to keep *some* connection between science and truth have developed various types of what we might call "soft" realism. We will look briefly at three types, which are not all mutually exclusive.

1. Limited realism. Limited realism is the position that, although realism is correct, not everything in any given theory is to be taken literally. For instance, some people believe that a theoretical term is legitimately considered as referring to real entities only if that term is important in more than one theory. The idea is that any set of phenomena can be theoretically explained in a number of alternative ways (noted above) and that the presence of some theoretical term in just one theory does not carry much weight. That theory could easily be mistaken. But if appeal to such a theoretical entity were completely mistaken, it would be unlikely that reference to that entity would be theoretically helpful in other domains of phenomena as well. The more areas it was helpful in, the less plausible it would be to maintain that the entity did not exist and that the term did not refer to it. Thus perhaps one should not take literally a term that occurred in only one scientific context, but one might be more justified in accepting the reality of such an entity if reference to it occurred essentially in a number of theories.

In related fashion, it is sometimes argued that scientific advancement is often not in the form of revolution, where an old theory is thrown out, but in the form of addition of a new theory correcting an old theory by restricting its scope and recasting the old theory as a limiting case of the new.[8] For instance, some scientists interpret Newtonian dynamics not as a theory exploded by relativity but as a limiting case (in low mass and velocity situations) of relativity. Further theories may restrict the scope of relativity, in which case relativity theory will become a limiting case of that newer theory. And so on. On this view, older theories become embedded or nested in successive shells of newer and newer theories, each one of which limits the scope of earlier ones. Some proponents of this view take the position that realism is justified with respect to the inner, embedded theories. Those "mature" theories, being strictly limited and having through those limitations survived subsequent scientific advances, can be taken as very likely true, although the newer, outer theories, whose correct scope may not yet be known and that may even be overthrown while leaving the core theories intact, are less legitimately taken as true. Here again we have a realism, although a realism applied only in certain cases.

I have suggested here the general features that hold for all types of limited realism: for the limited realist, not just any part of any theory is to be interpreted realistically, but some parts of some theories are.

2. Metaphoric realism. One motivation for some antirealist views has been the conviction (following Kuhn) that not all human subjectivity can be eradicated from science and the belief that since objective truth about the world is not human flavored, the subjectively tinged results of science could never truly match reality.

In recent decades, however, some realists have argued that theories may carry their truth in a way that (even admitting a subjective shading) does not preclude realism. How does that work? In normal talk we use a variety of devices to convey truth. Sometimes we try to speak the unvarnished, literal truth and intend our words to be taken at face value as when we report, "The tree is seven feet tall." Sometimes we speak in less literal ways, although we mean to be conveying truth nonetheless. For instance, when we speak of someone's iron will, we certainly do not mean that something immaterial (a will) is composed of something material (iron). Yet we do mean to be saying something revealing—and thus true—about the person in question. Some have argued that, in a similar way, talk about theoretical matters is meant to convey truth but a truth that is neither a purely literal rendering of our statement (contrary to a hard realism), nor a truth having to do just with purely observational matters (contrary to positivism), nor a merely subjective truth.

The truths in question are *metaphorical* truths.[9] In such cases we employ the concepts from one domain in a partially descriptive manner in another domain. Thus on this tempered realist view when we use a term from ordinary experience— "particle" or "wave"—in a theoretical context and with reference to something unobservable, we are saying something true but not completely literally descriptive, just as we are in applying a concept from one context *(iron)* in another domain entirely, with reference to someone's will.

Theoretical explanations, on this view, will therefore be *metaphoric redescriptions* of the theoretical reality in question. The concepts employed metaphorically will, of course, be concepts with which we are already familiar, and thus explanation and understanding will involve "reduction to the familiar."

Of course some aspects of a concept used metaphorically do not apply in the metaphorically described situation. When we say that someone has a will of iron, we do not imply that she should be concerned about rust. That part of the concept does not apply. Similarly, in the scientific case some aspects of the metaphorically employed concept will not apply to the theoretical matter in question. There will also be some aspects of the imported concept about which it will not be known whether or not they apply, and those aspects will suggest areas for further research to see whether they do in fact apply.

Whether metaphors can be wholly defined and replaced by more literal statements is a matter of some dispute among philosophers. But if our understanding of nature must be in terms of things familiar to us (and what alternative is there?), and if our familiar concepts do not quite fit the substructure of nature (and some physicists believe that results in quantum mechanics demonstrate that), then partial descriptions by way of metaphor may be a limitation we must accept. But that would not be to say that science did not discover truths or that our theories were incorrect. It would perhaps say only that our theories are unavoidably incomplete in ways we cannot anticipate. But since we have already seen the unavoidable tentativeness of science, this unavoidable partialness growing out of human limitations concerning what was or was not experienceable, thinkable or familiar would not be surprising.

3. Approximate truth. Some philosophers of science, reluctant to claim that we are the lucky ones who have finally gotten to the truth in some theoretical areas, nonetheless want to maintain that science has made theoretical progress over the years and that progress is in some way linked to truth. Our theories, on this view, are closer to truth, or more closely approximate truth, or have a greater verisimilitude, than did previous theories, although future theories may come closer yet. It is that *movement* toward truth that constitutes scientific theoretical progress, and it is the fact that it is toward *truth* that constitutes the realism of this position.[10]

Although attractive, this position raises difficult questions. First, exactly what might it mean to say that one theory more closely approximates truth than another? And second, under what conditions might we be justified in thinking that one theory did more closely approximate truth than another? Consider this case: suppose you have been appointed judge in a contest to see which of two people can guess most closely the number of beans in a jar. Both contestants guess, and you now must decide which one came closest. It would be easy, of course, if you knew the correct number. But if you do not, how do you decide? Now think of a scientific case. Suppose you have two theories before you, and you want to judge which is closest to the truth. You do not know what the true theory is. In fact, lack of that knowledge is what has driven you to turn to the idea of approximate truth to begin with. How do you decide?

It looks as though at the least one would have to have some theory about confirmation—a philosophical theory about the characteristics of scientific theories and their relationship to data on the one hand, about truth on the other, and about links between the two.

In fact, all varieties of realism depend on (or trip over) some concept of confirmation, and it is to confirmation that we now turn.

Confirmation

If realism has the advantages of conforming to what most practicing scientists have believed they were doing (thus restoring the explanatory power of science and accounting at least partially for the successes of extending theories into new domains of observation), it has, on the other hand, to face all the difficult problems of theoretical confirmation that antirealists sidestep.

It has been traditionally held that confirmation for any sort of scientific general principle must come by way of positive instances. (A positive instance of a principle is an instance that conforms to that principle. For example, a red ruby provides a positive instance of the generalization that all rubies are red.) We cannot, however, obtain positive instances of theoretical principles by direct observation, since with the theoretical we are dealing with the unobservable. One could obtain such instances indirectly if there were some rigorous, logical connection between observation and theory, but as we have seen, there is no such connection.

If we are to obtain positive instances of theoretical principles, it will have to be through correspondence rules.[11] Correspondence rules are principles stating connections between the observable and the theoretical, and it is through systems of correspondence rules that observation and theory bear on each other. Therefore, if we know the right correspondence rules, we will be able to associate observational occurrences with their corresponding theoretical occurrences, which, if the theoretical principles are correct, will provide positive instances of those principles.

So far so good. But that solution to the initial problem raises another. How are we to discover what theoretical matter is connected to what observational matter? How can we be confident that the correspondence rules we have accepted are right? In short, how are we to get *confirmation* of correspondence rules?

The initial suggestion might be this: look for positive instances of the correspondence rules. But there is a problem there, and to see what it is let us consider a parable.

Suppose your friend is a political prisoner and your only means of communication with him is by bribing a guard to relay messages. Suppose the messages are so important that you want to be sure the guard is reliable, that what she tells you the prisoner says really is what the prisoner says. How might you proceed? The reasonable way would be to talk to the prisoner directly and ask if he had said specific things the guard had related to you. If the prisoner said yes, then you would have positive instances of the guard's honesty, and you could be more confident in the message she brings. But in this case you *cannot* talk with the prisoner directly. The only way to ask him if he really said some specific thing is to ask the guard to ask him and then rely on the guard's report of his reply. But since the guard's reliability is the issue, you have made no noticeable progress. It looks as though your choice is either to have faith in the guard's reliability or not to have faith.

Trying to confirm correspondence rules seems to parallel that case closely. We have no access to unobservable objects, processes and events (the prisoner) *except* through correspondence rules (the guard), which relates the theoretical to things we can observe (the guard tells us what the prisoner says). If we wish to check on the accuracy of the correspondence rules, we need to determine what unobservable events take place (what the prisoner says), what observable events take place (what the guard says), and see if the two are related in the proper manner (see if the prisoner says what the guard says he says). But we have exactly the same problem as in the prisoner case; we have no direct access to the theoretical, so we cannot check the reliability of correspondence rules independently of the correspondence rules.

The process looks viciously circular. If confirmation of theoretical principles depends on correspondence rules and if confirmation of correspondence rules is impossible, then realism would appear to be as unacceptable as antirealism—a dilemma indeed, given that those seem to be the only real options.

The realist here faces a variety of other difficulties, but I shall mention just two more. When we take a realist view of theories, we are not just projecting regularities we have observed in a limited realm of experience and generalizing them, nor are we projecting them into other regions of space and time, as we are when dealing with empirical principles. We are projecting from experiences involving observables into the realm of unobservables, or making cross-level projections. But what reason do we have for thinking that we even have the right *concepts* for describing that unobservable level? And if theoretical explanation is reduction to the familiar, what reason do we have for thinking that unobservable things somehow parallel specific things with which we are familiar?

Horrible problems abound. It is generally admitted that there can be any number of distinct theories, all of which can explain any given body of data (underdetermination again). In fact, there can be distinct theories, theories postulating different entities, processes and so forth on the theoretical level, all of which have exactly the same observational consequences and make exactly all the same predictions. But if that is so, then *there can be no purely empirical or observational way of deciding which, if any, of those distinct theories is correct.* How then can we ever, even in principle, find out which is the right theory?

The above are difficult questions, and no one has complete answers to them. But philosophers of science have become increasingly willing to tackle them, since the alternative seems to be an antirealism increasingly seen as sterile. And not all of the above issues have proved to be totally intractable. Several of them have yielded to at least partial solutions, of which we shall briefly consider two.

First, there may be a way out of the prisoner-case/correspondence-rule impasse. Suppose that your prisoner was in contact with another prisoner, who was able to smuggle messages out through another guard. If you got a message through your guard and also got a message from your prisoner friend via the second prisoner through the second guard, then if the messages matched you would feel more confidence in the first guard, since her message matched another with which she had had no contact. Maybe she is reliable after all.

Of course that would not *prove* her reliability. Maybe the match of the messages was coincidence. Maybe she and the other guard are in cahoots. But if more and more such messages match, coincidence seems less and less likely. And if your prisoner is in contact (by way of the prisoners' underground) with another prisoner in some other country, and if he sends that other prisoner a message and that prisoner smuggles the message out through his guard (whom your guard does not even know), then if that message matches ones you are getting from your friend through the original guard, both coincidence and collusion seem increasingly unlikely. In short, it begins to seem more and more likely that the original guard is reliable.

There are exact parallels in the scientific case. Science involves networks of theoretical principles and correspondence rules related to each other and to observation in various ways. Thus it is often the case that distinct correspondence rules have connections, either direct or indirect, with the *same* theoretical matters. When that occurs, correspondence rules can be used to check each other, just as with the guards. And if two existing theories in entirely different areas (different countries) can be linked *theoretically* (the prisoners' underground), the observational implications (guards' reports) of the one can be used as a test of the theory and correspondence rules in the other area. The support for the correspondence rules provided in this case is even more impressive because the two theories and their correspondence rules arose independently. The meshing of their results was not originally built-in (the guards did not know each other and there was thus no collusion).

All this is metaphorical and general, but the intuitions can be made tighter,[12] and many philosophers of science now believe that the problem of confirmation of correspondence rules does not involve a *vicious* circularity.

What of the problem of multiple distinct theories all having the same empirical consequences? In such cases, decisions between competing theories cannot be made on a purely empirical basis and, if they are to be made at all, must involve other factors. Many philosophers of science believe that several such factors bear on the acceptability of a theory. For instance, a theory empirically adequate but simple is to be preferred to a more complicated one, although there is no consensus over what simplicity involves. A theory fitting well with other established theories is to be preferred to one that does not. A theory giving rise to unexpected discoveries thereby gains ground. A theory fruitful in suggesting new lines of research or new experiments is taken as better than one that does not. Recent lists of desiderata for theories have also included observational nesting (allowing a theory to retain the theoretical and empirical successes of the theory it succeeds), track record (how successful it has been in handling problems in the past), smoothness (ability to incorporate necessary changes in some organic, non-ad-hoc fashion), internal consistency and compatibility with well-grounded metaphysical beliefs.[13]

Why should theories exhibiting those characteristics be preferable to theories that do not? Because those desiderata are taken to be *epistemic* values, values that figure into scientific decisions and evaluations of theories and that are taken to be truth-tending in the sense that decisions made in light of those values are *more likely* to result in movement closer to truth than those that do not. It is argued that science has progressed historically by virtue of employing such values and that that success can be explained in part because such values nudge science toward the truth and the closer a theory is to the truth the more successful and powerful it will be.[14]

Of course, adopting such criteria involves a departure from the purely empirical. But as we have seen, the idea that science is purely empirical represents a serious misconception in any case.

Enormous problems remain in the area of confirmation. It is never conclusive. Neither is disconfirmation. It is not even clear how to assess the impact of specific instances on the theories of which they are instances. There may never be a logic of confirmation. But the basic weaknesses of antirealism have made philosophers of science reluctant to avoid the difficulties of confirmation theory at the cost of accepting an antirealism. The basic strengths of realism—faithfulness to what most scientists have believed they were doing, allowing us to make sense of the surprising predictions theories sometimes make, accounting for the success of science historically and providing explanatory power—have made philosophers of science willing to face such problems.[15]

And even if there could not in principle be any rigorous solutions to the above problems, that would not necessarily be an overwhelming problem. We ought perhaps to keep in mind the Kuhnian lesson that science is a deeply human pursuit. And rigor may not be the ultimate wellspring of human activity.

The general conclusion then is that science is capable of discovering truths concerning objective, independent, real matters beyond the direct scope both of our observation and of observability, that theories we arrive at may be true, that it is often rational to believe them to be true (or at least approximately true), and that science can produce theoretical knowledge. That is not to say that the process is automatic, foolproof and unmolded by the foibles of humans and their subjectivity. It is not. But there seems little reason to think that it ought to be, or that that should bar us either from truth or from knowing.

6

The Limitations of Science
What Can It Not Tell Us?

It *is just as important to know what science cannot tell us as to* know what it can. Much that is said in this chapter should be obvious. That makes the fact that it needs saying all the more appalling. But in the modern era, much that ought to be obvious has been forgotten, denied or ignored.

One limitation of science is its inability to provide *proof* of its results. Although scientific theories are always less than absolutely certain, that limitation is not a limitation on the *scope* of science. But if any part of reality lies outside the boundaries imposed on science by its methods, that part of reality will be beyond the competence of science; and if knowledge is artificially restricted to scientific knowledge, we will thus be sheltering ourselves and our beliefs from the relevant portions of reality.

Foundations of Science

Our initial question must be this: Are there areas within which pure science cannot directly speak? There are many. To begin with, science cannot validate either scientific method itself or the presuppositions of that method. Consider, for instance, the principle of the uniformity of nature. As discussed earlier this principle does not appear to be a *result* of science for the simple reason that it is a *presupposition* employed in generating results. Observations and data are interpreted in the light of that presupposition. That interpretive role is evidenced by the protected status the uniformity principle has. When things do not go as demanded by our latest theories, we do not conclude that nature has changed the rules since yesterday. Rather we conclude that our theories went off the trolley somewhere.

Similar remarks apply to other foundational presuppositions of science. One has to make some assumptions in order to have a place to start, just as in geometry one cannot construct proofs without axioms. The axioms are not themselves results of the system. They are the pegs on which the system hangs and without which there would be no system at all. Similarly with science there must be some methodological presuppositions with which to begin, and those presuppositions are not generated out of science itself. (There is feedback; sometimes scientific results or lack of results where expected induce people to reexamine foundational principles, but those reexaminations are substantially philosophical rather than purely scientific.)[1]

If we then are justified in accepting the foundational principles of science (that is, if accepting those foundations is legitimate or rational), then justification must rest on something other than scientific method. Thus either accepting science itself is not justifiable or else there is some nonscientific, justifiable basis for accepting science. Thus not only can science not validate its own foundations (implying that there *are* areas outside the competence of science), but if we do accept science, including its foundations, there must be some other sort of grounds for accepting at least some beliefs. This implies that science cannot be the only legitimate basis for believing something. Those who claim either that science is competent for dealing with all matters or that science is the only legitimate method for dealing with any matter are seriously confused.

Ultimate Origins

Given that we can only rationally accept science so long as we are prepared to admit that the competence of science is not universal, what areas might lie beyond the legitimate scope of science?

First, science cannot give any ultimate naturalistic or mechanical explanation for the existence of the universe with which it deals. Physicists currently talk about fluctuations in a vacuum somehow snowballing and resulting in the universe. As one physicist recently explained, "Our universe is simply one of those things which happen from time to time."[2] But that does not yet explain why the vacuum should have such characteristics as to make such fluctuations either possible or productive of a universe. To explain that, one needs prior principles. To scientifically explain those prior principles one must have prior prior principles, and to explain those one must have yet earlier principles, and so on. Ultimately one must just take some foundational principles as given, and those givens will *a fortiori* not be either generated or explained by science.

Some physicists, impressed by the deep connections between observer and observed according to some interpretations of quantum mechanics, have advanced various forms of the anthropic principle mentioned earlier, a principle that tries to tie the fact that we are here to various constraints on the basic physics of the universe.[3]

Whether one finds such attempts promising or not, it can be seen that when questions such as those of ultimate origins arise, scientific method cannot be effectively applied. In the face of that inapplicability, some maintain that we cannot fruitfully investigate such questions at all. In short, if scientific method does not work there, we cannot escape from sheer speculation, subjectivity, prejudice and ignorance. Common as that position is, we have already seen that it is incorrect. If science itself is legitimate and can be rationally accepted, then since it cannot validate itself, there has to be some *other* legitimate means of validation. The price of holding out for science as the only legitimate basis for belief is the illegitimacy of science itself, and that seems too high a price.

Ultimate Purpose

Science also typically does not address questions of the ultimate purpose of our existence or of the universe. Why? It is tempting to say simply that purposes cannot be observed and thus cannot be addressed by the methods of natural science, which are tied to observation. But science almost routinely and quite properly deals with things not directly observable even in principle—electrons, quarks, fields and so forth. (Although scientists often talk about observing such things, their sense of "observation" is not what we ordinarily mean.) Therefore, mere unobservability does not disqualify something from proper science. Of course, those theoretical entities and processes are tied to the empirical through networks of correspondence rules, but there seems to be no reason in principle why one could not link purposes to observables.

In fact, we all routinely *do* connect observations to conclusions about *human* purposes, intentions and so forth. Our dealings with other people depend on our having beliefs about their purposes, intentions and states of mind, and we often acquire those beliefs in the course of, say, *observing* them boot their philosophy text out of the window. Historically, purpose (or teleology) was a primary explanatory and interpretive category in science. The connections between underlying purposes and observable things were perceived as being strong enough to allow the empirical study of nature to be a source of knowledge about God. Tracing such connections was a popular project for scientists until well into the nineteenth century.

However, the concept of purpose fell into scientific disfavor. One major reason was that purpose came to be viewed as scientifically less fruitful than more naturalistic explanations of natural phenomena. It was not that trying to explain things by reference to ultimate purpose was inherently irrational or that purposes could not in principle be connected to observation, but that scientists came to believe they were better able to tie loose ends together, to predict, and to see how things worked by trying to account for physical things and events along mechanistic, naturalistic lines—lines that made no *immediate* appeal to God's activity, purposes and so forth. Hence, "natural" science.

Of course, the fact that science generally does not make use of the concept of ultimate purposes in no way suggests it is not meaningful or important.

Reductions

Restricting science in practice to naturalistic concepts is perhaps all right so long as one realizes what one is doing and so long as one does not then try, in the name of science, to force such restrictions onto areas for which purely naturalistic concepts are inadequate or inappropriate. A method of investigation deliberately restricted to the naturalistic (or the purely material or mechanistic) will not be competent to deal with most of the fundamental questions of morality and value, psychology, theology and religion, philosophy and some other areas as well.

Most philosophers and scientists have recognized these limitations, but others have objected to the idea of science being limited. (There are various motivations behind that dislike, but some of the reasons have had an antireligious flavor.) Those who restrict science to the material but wish the authority and competence of science to be unlimited have responded in one of two ways to claims that natural science cannot accommodate the concepts of ethics, philosophy, theology and so on. The first has been to simply deny the significance of such concepts, arguing that they are unimportant or perhaps even incoherent. The other response has been to admit the legitimacy of such notions but to try to correct their "deficiencies" by molding (or warping) them into shapes conforming to what were taken to be the demands of natural science.

The first position was widely popular among positivists but cannot really be taken seriously. For one thing, any theory of meaning implying that the sentence "murder is morally wrong" is not only not true but does not even have meaning, has provided its own refutation.

The second of the two alternatives (taken by those who lay claim to expanded areas of competence for natural science) takes different forms depending on the specific area science is expanded into. But there is one characteristic they all have in common: if the methods of natural science as now practiced are indeed inappropriate for those areas, then extending natural science into them will inevitably involve a reduction at some point, and some segment of reality will get distorted and deformed as it is forced into an inappropriate conceptual cage.

Let us look briefly at how such an extension of science (or reduction of reality) works in the specific cases of morality.

Attempts to investigate morality "scientifically" have been fairly popular in some circles during this century. One of the better known proponents was the anthropologist Ruth Benedict.[4] Her presupposition was that if there was anything of significance in ethics, it would have to be something discoverable by "trained observers." Consequently, concepts such as *right, wrong, moral* or *immoral* applied (if at all) only to things that anthropologists could identify through empirical cultural studies.

But of course one cannot directly observe the wrongness or rightness of an action, at least not with the physical senses. One can observe actions that are wrong or perhaps see them *as* wrong, but the wrongness per se of the action is not part either of one's sensory reports or the printout of one's measuring devices. What then can the anthropologist observe? Primarily he or she can determine what the members of some culture believe, prefer, praise, condemn and so forth. In short, the trained observer can discover cultural patterns of human attitudes. And there are difficulties even there. But if moral concepts have to be constructed from the observable, and if what is relevantly observable are human attitudes, then morality quite quickly becomes a matter of human attitude. What is moral is what a culture approves. What is immoral is what a culture disapproves. Further, since different cultures seem to exhibit different attitudes, we are driven to the conclusion that morality itself (and not merely moral *beliefs*) varies. The ultimate result is an ethical subjective relativism.

Subjective relativism is popular and has several major attractions. For instance, if morality is dependent solely on human opinion, then we do not have to worry about being held responsible to a divine standard. We do not have to worry that our moral beliefs may be mistaken; our believing something to be right makes it right. So it really does not matter what we believe, as long as we are sincere. Convenient indeed.

However, in addition to problems from a Christian perspective this subjective relativism collapses in a way somewhat parallel to positivism. A question naturally arising in the context of subjective relativism is, what if some person thinks it is right for him to slaughter all his neighbors? A standard response is that it would be *socially* disapproved, thus wrong even if some individual thinks otherwise. But what if some *society* thinks that slaughtering their neighboring societies (or a minority within their own society) is morally permissible? (That is not unheard of historically.) Does it not then become okay for them to set about doing it?

The only tenable rejoinder for subjective relativists seems to be this: that inflicting gratuitous harm on others is wrong no matter who you or your society are or what you think. But that response breaks the link between the moral concept *wrong* and the observable (the attitude of the society). If that link is broken then the whole project is compromised, since the project depended on tying moral concepts to observables.[5]

Apparently the only way to make palatable the results of this type of extension of science into ethics is to abandon the underlying principle at a crucial point; and that seems to indicate that, even from a purely philosophical standpoint, the extension of a natural science into ethics in this way is mistaken.

Other examples could be given as well (philosophy, psychology, theology), but the patterns are clear. Natural science has its limitations, and pushing it into areas beyond those lines comes at the cost of violence to the invaded area and without much particular profit—especially if one has an outdated conception of science, as those behind such attempts almost always do.

What sets those other areas off both from natural science and from each other is the applicability of characteristic descriptive and explanatory concepts not appropriate to purely natural science but essential to the area in question. For instance, one cannot do justice to ethics without concepts of *right* and *wrong* (and *justice*). In explaining human actions we often have to appeal to human *reasons*. Theology loses its content if one is not allowed to talk of God, sin and salvation. And all three areas require the notion of *responsibility*.

Can those and other concepts be *reduced* to concepts of natural science? Can those explanations be reduced to explanations of natural science? The answer seems to be no. It seems relatively obvious that the concept of *moral responsibility,* for instance, is simply a different concept than any that can be put together from the resources of purely natural science. The same holds for the key concepts of other areas as well. None of the specific attempts at such reductions has worked.

There is one other cluster of limitations affecting science even within its own proper domain, the impacts of which are difficult to assess. These are those limitations that result from the fact that it is humans who do science. The doing of science depends on human fundamental intuitions concerning what is or is not conceptually possible and what is or is not conceptually linked to what else. It depends on a variety of human normative concepts such as what is *good* evidence, what conclusions can be *rationally* drawn and what is the *right* way to proceed. It depends on human thought processes, on human perceptual abilities, on the limits of human concepts, on available technology, on available funding (which often depends on the quirks of politics).

In none of those areas do we have any good reason to be confident of our infallibility, and even if we had some such guarantee of our ability to avoid error and distortion, there is not much reason to think that we would invariably make *use* of that ability. It would be nice if we had some compartment of our lives into which our fallenness and finitude did not intrude, but the case for science being such an area is yet to be made.

7

"Scientific" Challenges to Religious Belief

S*cience has limitations, and various sorts of intellectual disasters* ensue if those limitations are ignored. In a slightly different way science has been taken as a basis for various philosophical challenges to religious belief. In this chapter we will look in varying depth at four challenges—that religious belief is defective in not being scientific, that it is defective in not being provable, that it is defective in that there is no (or insufficient) evidence for it and that it is scientifically superfluous. We will then briefly discuss who can or cannot legitimately raise such challenges and conclude with some general observations about challenges.

Four Challenges
1. Religious belief is not scientific. Whether or not the charge that religious belief is not scientific is even true depends on what *scientific* means, and as we have seen, that is a matter of dispute. But suppose

that religious belief is not scientific. Why is that an objection? Presumably because it is presupposed that anything not scientific is suspect, unreasonable, false or the like. But why accept that presupposition?[1] Is the belief that I exist scientific? I certainly have neither acquired nor tested that belief on the basis of sensory evidence. After all, if that belief depended on what I could sense, I would have to assume my own existence at the outset in order to believe that I was having the relevant sensory experience, which would make the whole process hopelessly circular. But if belief in my own existence is unscientific in some sense, then so much the worse for any principle saying there is something suspect about any belief that is not scientific.

And of course, the principle that anything not scientific is suspect undercuts itself. It seems clear that that principle is a philosophical, not a scientific, principle and consequently declares itself to be illegitimate. The objection therefore seems fairly seriously misguided.

2. Religious belief is unprovable. Another popular challenge is that since religious beliefs cannot be proved, they are suspect or irrational, or at least suffer by comparison with scientific beliefs.

That challenge, however, presupposes that beliefs that are unprovable are less than first class. Since neither scientific beliefs nor our common everyday beliefs are susceptible to strict proofs, this principle would rule them out along with religious beliefs. But we need not fear this principle; since it is not provable, it declares itself suspect or irrational, thereby undercutting any objections based on it.

3. Religious belief is unsupported by evidence. Another fairly popular charge is that there is no evidence for the basic religious beliefs, combined with the further claim that it is not rational to believe anything not based on evidence. The perception that science demands evidence for what it accepts is part of what makes this view attractive.

To see exactly what is involved, we need to look more closely at the relationship between theories and evidence. Suppose that in 1900 someone had suggested that atoms could be split into smaller parts or that several atoms could be squashed together to form a single larger one. Given then-current views that atoms were indestructible, the idea would probably have been rejected. In fact, most scientists would probably have claimed that there was no evidence to support such a view. But in a sense there was shining evidence for such a view: it rose every morning and set every evening. If atoms were immutable, there would be no sunshine. Thus the very existence of sunshine was powerful evidence for the mutability of atoms.

But of course, in 1900 no one knew that. No one knew that sunshine was evidence of mutability for the simple reason that no one knew of any theory that connects the generating of sunlight with that mutability. If no one knows the connection between two things, the one cannot be reasonably claimed to be evidence for the other. It is only after the connection is known (or at least suspected) that such claims are justified. In general what we *perceive* to be evidence and what we *take* it to be evidence for is relative to the background theories we accept. (Recall that one of the difficulties with the Baconian view of science was that it missed just this point, thinking that evidence was always evidence per se, declaring to us what it was evidence for.)

Now the Christian might, for instance, hold that the existence of a world, or the existence of life, or her own existence, or perhaps some sorts of experiences she has had, can best be explained by reference to certain religious principles or to a Creator. She believes that those things constitute evidence for her beliefs. When the religious critic says that there is no evidence, he certainly does not mean to be denying the existence of the world, or of life, or of himself, but is serving notice that he does not accept the background principles that give evidential status to those things. By claiming that there is no evidence, then, the critic is really saying in effect that the background principles that a believer holds—for instance, that there could not have been a world had it not been for a Creator—are false.

It would be interesting to see, for instance, the critic's evidence that universes could occur independently of being created. (And is he not asserting the importance of evidence?) If universes could not occur independently, then the existence of this one would certainly be evidence—conclusive evidence, in fact—for theistic belief. But the critic's claim that there is no evidence implies that any principle connecting existence to createdness is false and that no one will know of any such connection, ever. What is his evidence for that sweeping claim? The existence of this universe? But that helps his case only on the assumption that this one is uncreated, which is part of the issue. If he has no evidence for that position, then in holding it he is violating the very principle of "no belief without evidence" that he is trying to use against the Christian.

In any case, what is important to realize here is that despite appearances the dispute is really not a dispute over evidence but over background principles relevant to the interpretation of things everyone accepts. By making it sound as though it is a question of evidence that is either there or not there, the critic makes his charge sound much more substantial than it is.

But what of the principle that one should not believe anything except on the basis of evidence? Taking that principle seriously gets one into rather severe difficulties. If one believes something on the basis of evidence, then one presumably has to believe that the evidence is reliable. But if one can only believe things on the basis of evidence, then one must have evidence for one's evidence. But of course, if one can only believe things on the basis of evidence, then one must have evidence for one's evidence for one's evidence. The chain, as you can see, is going to get a bit unwieldy. If that sequence does not ever end, then all beliefs will be ultimately illegitimate— including the belief that one should have evidence for one's beliefs. (And incidentally, what *is* the evidence for that principle itself?) It looks as though there are only two ways out of this difficulty for the critic. Either he can claim that all of one's beliefs should ultimately be based on beliefs that provide their own evidence for themselves (however that is supposed to work), or he can give up the general form of his principle and claim that there are some beliefs that can be rationally believed without evidence.

If the challenger takes the first route, then we have to find out what sorts of beliefs provide their own evidence, and here the challenger is entering a philosophical thicket. It might just be that some religious beliefs are in that category, in which case the present criticism of religious belief would fail because there *would* be evidence for those beliefs; they would provide their own evidence. If the challenger takes the other route, then we have to find out what sorts of beliefs can be rationally accepted without evidence, and here the challenger is entering another philosophical thicket. It might just be that some religious beliefs are in that category, in which case the present criticism of religious belief would fail because those beliefs would be exempt from the critic's requirement that they be supported by evidence. In this case, the critic would have to give up the criticism unless he could show that even though some beliefs can be properly accepted without evidence, no religious belief is among them. *Showing* that is going to be difficult. And if, rather than trying to show that to be true, the objector simply insists on taking it as true without evidence, it appears we are dealing with a case of simple prior prejudice being supported by ad hoc (even "unscientific") means.[2]

4. *Religious belief is superfluous.* Another challenge is that, in the face of scientific advance, religious belief is superfluous. Science, it is said, has consistently taken over more and more of the territory once occupied by religious beliefs. For instance, it was once thought that the stars and planets were moved by supernatural agency. Now we have a naturalistic explanation. It was once thought that the diversity of living organisms required supernatural agency. Scientists now give naturalistic explanations. And so on. Religion, so the argument goes, flourishes in the gaps of naturalistic explanations, and as science continues to fill in those gaps, there will eventually be no place left. It will then be seen that natural law reigns supreme, and there will be naturalistic explanations for everything.

There are two parts to this challenge. First is an inductive argument that since past gaps in our understanding of the world have been filled by naturalistic explanations, all remaining gaps can ultimately be similarly filled in. Second is a principle that naturalistic explanations take precedence over other explanations, making other sorts of explanations superfluous. Let us look at each part.

To begin with, since the argument in the first part is inductive, and since inductive arguments do not establish their conclusions with certainty, we are not dealing with a *proof* here. Besides that, not *all* past gaps have been closed naturalistically for the simple reason that not all such gaps have been closed at all. There are still some longstanding scientific mysteries. Worse yet, Kuhn argues that science sometimes loses some ground in revolutions; if that is correct, gaps once closed may be reopened when the theory that formerly closed the gap is overturned. Thus, even if all known gaps were closed by naturalistic theories, there is no guarantee that they would stay closed.

A further weakness of the argument emerges in light of common scientific procedure. Even when a scientific theory is admitted by scientists to be inadequate, it will generally not be discarded unless there is an acceptable alternative theory available. It is generally a matter of practical policy among scientists that "acceptable" means (among other things) "naturalistic." Thus even if the correct alternative to an inadequate theory was a nonnaturalistic theory (for instance, a theory citing God's direct activity), scientists would either refuse to give up the old theory that was *known* to be incorrect or would move to some different naturalistic theory that (on the present hypothesis) was also incorrect, although perhaps not yet known to be so. Science is often credited with being a self-corrective enterprise—and to an extent it is. But if part of reality lies beyond the natural realm, then science cannot get at that truth without abandoning the naturalism it presently follows as a methodological rule of thumb.

Therefore, for all science can tell, difficulties it has already run into are difficulties requiring nonnatural solutions. The fact that science as presently practiced could not recognize that even if it were true makes the claim that science has not yet recognized any nonnatural gaps less consequential than it might otherwise be.

Further, some philosophers of science (including Kuhn) believe that no scientific theory or paradigm ever solves all the problems it defines for itself. If that is correct, then there being things that science cannot account for (gaps) is not a temporary situation that can in principle be overcome in the future but is endemic to science. That amounts to a denial that scientific accounts of reality are ever absolutely complete.

Incompleteness in scientific naturalistic accounts of reality does seem unavoidable. Suppose we could explain every event in the world by reference to some set of natural laws. Since the operation of those laws would be an important feature of reality, we could ask why those laws held. The response could be either that those laws were just "brute fact" or that some deeper-level natural laws explained the set of laws in question, or some principles outside the normal scope of science (theological, for instance) could be cited. But the first response is no explanation at all, the second merely pushes the question back a step (so providing no *complete* scientific explanation), and most would see the third as going beyond the scientific (so providing no complete *scientific* naturalistic explanation on the usual definition of "scientific"). It is thus an implication of most views of science that explanations within the natural realm can apparently be either complete or scientific but not both simultaneously.

But if such incompleteness is unavoidable, then the conclusion of the inductive argument—that eventually all gaps in our understanding of reality can be filled naturalistically—cannot be true even in principle.

The second part of this challenge, the principle that naturalistic explanations take precedence over other explanations, is not above suspicion either. Why, if one had a naturalistic explanation of something and a nonnaturalistic explanation of that same thing, should one automatically be obliged first to choose between them (implying that they are competitors), and second, to give priority to the naturalistic one? What is the argument for that competition and that priority, or are those simply someone's philosophical preferences?

This whole challenge presupposed that religious beliefs as well as any divine activity in the world must find refuge in the gaps of scientific explanation and causes. But many, many Christians reject that view, seeing God as working in this world sometimes in a direct way but more often working *through* his laws rather than in the fortunate (or unfortunate) cracks between them. If God designed his laws to accomplish his purposes, why should we see him then as being in competition with those laws, so that we have to choose between God's activities and natural laws as somehow rival explanations?

This challenge, then, seems not only philosophically weak but perhaps not very accurate theologically either.

The Challengers

As we have seen, many of the challenges purportedly based on science are not powerful. But the situation for "scientific" critics of religious belief is even more difficult than the weakness of those challenges would indicate, for many of those critics could not legitimately raise many of the challenges even if the challenges did not involve obvious mistakes.

For instance, if one wishes to use theoretical results against religion, one must at least take theoretical results to be true. That simple fact prevents instrumentalists, who do not think that "true" applies to theoretical scientific results, from employing that sort of challenge.

Positivists in general are in much the same boat. They may try to cause difficulties with various of their philosophical principles, such as the verifiability criterion of meaning, but given their view that what science properly deals with are patterns within the observable, they can raise objections only if there is some purely observational result of science that is contrary to religious belief. But what pattern within purely observational matters does any major religion fundamentally deny? Most disputes (over, say, determinism, mechanism, evolution) have been either purely philosophical or else have concerned the theoretical interpretation of observational data. But the positivists, in insisting that the theoretical is really just disguised observational talk, have effectively fenced themselves out of any debate in which theoretical interpretations are taken seriously.

Radical subjectivists cannot make much of a splash here either. Remember that differing paradigms are allegedly incommensurable. That means that, on hard-line views, the contents of one paradigm many have no bearing on the contents of a differing one. Thus there will be no scientific results that everyone is rationally obliged to accept. If things in my paradigm are flatly out of alignment with things in your paradigm, your theories might not even provide the basis for a challenge to my science, much less a basis for a challenge to my religious beliefs. And if one further accepts the view that truth has no place in science, then science could not claim to have some particular *truth* by reference to which anything else, including religious belief, could be seen to be *false*.

It therefore looks as though only the realist can use scientific theory as a basis for criticism of religious belief. Others must restrict themselves to basing objections on philosophical presuppositions (which cannot be claimed to be *scientific* objections) or on empirical observations or generalizations; and most radicals and postmoderns cannot even do that, since according to most such views different people have different observations and there is no one system—not even one *world*—obligatory for everyone. Despite common claims, "scientific" criticisms of religion are often either general and philosophical, often based on uncritical use of outmoded positivist principles or just plain misconstruals of what science can and cannot do.

Concerning Challenges

As we will see later, some commentators on science believe that scientific beliefs and religious beliefs reside in such separate categories that they cannot even in principle come into conflict. If such views are correct, then any challenge to religious belief allegedly coming from science can be dismissed out of hand as mistaken.

It ought not be forgotten that science is a tentative and human pursuit. Frequently theories and observation do not quite match up. Sometimes deeply fundamental and commonly held presuppositions of science are brought into apparent conflict both with nature and with each other. The history of quantum mechanics is a case study of such conflict. When that happens, human choices concerning what to keep and what to abandon must eventually be made, and there is no ironclad logic for making those choices. The choices are constrained choices. They are not arbitrary, anything-goes leaps. But they are human choices, colored by the things that human choices are subject to. Given the track record of past human choices, even within science, we have to admit at least the outside possibility that some of the past choices now incorporated into our contemporary science were not exactly on target.

The results of science—often correct and often tremendously highly probable—are in principle not absolutely beyond question, not beyond any possibility of error. As we have seen, the way science proceeds guarantees that tentativeness in principle.

Thus even *if* challenges to religion could be properly raised, and even *if* they looked exceedingly powerful, believers would still not be obliged to wave white flags and turn their ultimate concern to the perfect tan.

Consider a parallel case. Suppose that someone presented you with a powerful, properly constituted scientific case for the conclusion that you did not have a body. Suppose that you could find no flaw in the case. You would still be best advised to put clothes on, for the simple reason that the belief that you have a body seems more certain than any scientific case that you did not, and it would appear the more reliable of the two. We might not know where the mistake in such a case was, but it would certainly not be irrational to conclude that there was a mistake somewhere or other. We would have a conflict in belief, and it would be reasonable to stick with the more evident, the more direct, the more firmly held of the competitors.[3]

Or if your neighbor presents you with an apparently flawless scientific case that you do not really exist, do not get too rattled if you cannot find any obvious mistakes in the case. They are there. After all, you have to exist for him to present the case to *you* at all.

The point is that scientific cases, although often quite powerful, are not conclusive cases. There are some areas in which even apparently powerful and flawless scientific cases would be refuted by the very fact that they go against things that we know even more directly, firmly and deeply than we can know those theoretical matters.

We can transfer that moral directly to the religious case. If you are presented with an apparently powerful scientific case against religion or against belief in God (which, again, some would rule out even in principle by reference to limitations of science), even if you cannot find specific mistakes, you are under no more of an obligation to surrender before such a case than you would be in the two examples presented above. If you know that God exists, then you also know that something—some human inference, some human interpretation, some human choice—has gone wrong somewhere in the scientific case, just as it has in the previous examples.

Another Question

Contrary to some claims, science does not appear to provide significant resources for assaults upon basic religious belief as such. But that suggests a further question: can science even in principle provide resources in support of any sort of religious belief? One aspect of that general issue—specifically, intelligent design theory—has recently generated rather heated debate. It is to this theory that we now turn.

8

Design &
Science

*I*t could be a scene straight out of *Star Trek. A doctor examining a* crew member who has fallen mysteriously ill discovers something remarkable in samples taken from the patient. What she finds is a tiny, self-contained, self-sustaining unit tightly packed with even tinier sub-units, which is controlled by what appear to be software and processors so compact and condensed that their components are specialized, complex individual molecules. Further, the doctor discovers, this microscopic entity contains a propulsion system driven by a nifty, minute, inboard electric rotary motor. The motor is attached to an outboard component which it rotates, thereby generating the propulsion. Although the entity is obviously not of human manufacture, the doctor recognizes an intelligently designed micro machine when she sees one. And though she does not yet know who designed it, what its purpose is or how it got into the crew member, she immediately issues a security alert.

That might have been a scene from *Star Trek,* but it is not. It is a story about *us*. Each of us has millions of these remarkable units in our own bodies—they are microorganisms called *E. coli*. Although *E. coli* are common parts of our natural internal and external environments, it is difficult not to be rather astonished by the existence of the microscopic electric rotary motors. In most contexts we (like the doctor) would take the existence of such a motor—complete with organic rotors, stators, bushings, driveshafts—as virtually conclusive evidence that some intelligent designer had been at work here. In fact, a number of scientists (e.g., Michael Behe, author of *Darwin's Black Box*) have come to exactly that conclusion and maintain that we cannot have a complete *scientific* understanding of some parts of nature without incorporating the concept of *design*. However, other scientists have come to exactly the opposite conclusion. For example, the subtitle of *The Blind Watchmaker* by Richard Dawkins is "Why the evidence of evolution reveals a universe without design." Dawkins's position is not merely that we do not need the concept of design to properly explain nature (even including bacterial electric rotary motors) but that a correct scientific understanding of nature *establishes* the *absence* of deliberate design in nature.

Obviously the issue of whether or not there is genuine, scientific evidence of intelligent design in nature will have extremely important implications. So how should we think about this issue? Historically, most people (including scientists) have believed that there was an active mind (or minds) behind the visible face of nature and that some (or all) visible things and events were results of and thus evidence of the intentions and activity of that mind (minds). Nature, as most saw it, was deliberately *planned, directed* or *designed*. From that perspective, *reasons, ideas, plans, thoughts, patterns* and *design* would all factor into the causal history, structure and function of things, and thus any adequate scientific account of nature would have to involve reference to those factors. That perspective was visible in the new science of the sixteenth and seventeenth centuries[1] and was given explicit expression in the Natural Theology movement of the eighteenth and early nineteenth centuries.

The idea that science can uncover evidence of deliberate design in the cosmos, and especially the idea that *supernatural design* can figure in truly scientific accounts of natural phenomena, subsequently fell on hard times. Such ideas are now generally viewed as scientifically illegitimate or worse. In tracking some of the issues involved we will begin by examining the basic concept of design, look next at some of the reasons underlying the widespread scientific ban on the concept of supernatural design in science, then look briefly at a current attempt to reintroduce the concept into science.

Design: Concept Basics

1. Artifacts. Activities of human agents typically leave visible traces on the world—traces we are generally able to recognize as resulting from human activity. For instance, when we come across a diesel bulldozer, we recognize that humans had a hand in that machine's coming into existence. That recognition is based in part upon our knowing some things about nature's capabilities and our recognition that nature unaided by agent activity would not or could not have produced any such phenomenon. In the production and properties of diesel bulldozers, things or events involved have been pushed in a direction contrary to the normal flow of nature—they exhibit what I shall call *counterflow*. And since nature unaided by agency could not or would not have produced any such thing, agency (in this case, human agency) was obviously involved. Things that unaided nature could not or would not produce and in whose production finite agents (humans, aliens, whatever) played some role we classify as *artifacts*.

We often recognize artifactuality even if we have no idea who or what the agents involved were, what they had in mind, what (if anything) their purpose was or how they produced the phenomenon in question. We could do so in some cases even if (contrary to the diesel bulldozer example) we had previously neither seen any such object nor seen any such object produced. For example, if the first humans ever to set foot on Mars discovered a huge stainless steel exact replica of Stonehenge, they could tell from its counterflow characteristics that it was an undoubted *artifact*. And if they knew further that they were the first humans on Mars, they could also confidently conclude that it was an *alien* artifact. That would be a perfectly reasonable—even "scientific"—conclusion, even if the identity, intentions, purposes and methods of the alien agents involved were completely unknown.

Artifactual and *designed* are not, however, synonymous. Someone whittling idly on a stick and paying no mind whatever to what she was doing would still produce a recognizable artifact, but that artifact would not be in any strong sense designed since its key characteristics were not intentionally produced.

But although it comes close, *intentionally produced artifactuality* is not yet quite the same as designedness. An artist might deliberately and painstakingly produce an exact replica of a suburban garbage heap, perhaps as some sort of social commentary. Although both the original and the replica would be unmistakable artifacts exhibiting undeniable counterflow, and although the replica would be an intentionally produced artifact, neither of them would on its own exhibit any properties constituting any marks of design in any intuitive sense.[2] So exactly what is design?

2. Design. A design is an *intentionally produced (or exemplified) pattern,* where a *pattern* is an abstract structure that resonates, matches or meshes in certain ways with *mind,* with *cognition.* That structure can be exemplified in an object, an event, a sequence of events or other phenomena, either material or abstract. For instance, the SETI program (the Search for ExtraTerrestrial Intelligence) looks for electromagnetic artifacts (alien microwave signals) representing deliberate alien attempts at communication—broadcasts of prime number sequences in binary code, for instance, as in the movie *Contact.*[3] Such a signal would clearly be a *designed* artifact—an intentionally produced pattern that nature on its own would not produce. And we would easily recognize it as such because of its very obvious *cognitive* character and content—its resonating with mind in a particularly evident way.[4]

There are several other possible categories of *resonating* as well. A hammer, for instance, is a designed artifact. In this case the resonating with mind consists in the correspondence between its actual artifactual characteristics and those required for fulfilling its intended purpose. A similar type of correspondence between the properties living organisms have and the properties they need in order to thrive in their environments—a matching typically referred to as the "adaptation of means to ends"—was frequently cited in the past as evidence of design in nature.

3. Agent activity. Since design involves the *deliberate* production of pattern, there is always agent activity somewhere in its history. Sometimes that activity is quite direct, sometimes not. Here is a simple analogy. Someone might carve a model wooden ship by hand *or* might construct some high tech machine that would turn out carved model ships automatically. The agent, the person, must *do* something in both cases. But in the one case the activity is direct—and anyone watching the wood being turned into a model would see it. In the other case, with respect to the actual carving of the ship the agent activity is only indirect. Anyone watching the wood being turned into a model ship would see only the completely mechanical, law-driven, automatic operation of a purely physical machine. There would have to be direct agent activity *somewhere*, but in this case it would be directed toward the making of the machine itself—or the machine that made the machine (or perhaps even further back).

4. Gaps. Whenever humans, aliens or other finite beings act to produce artifacts (or design), marks of that activity—counterflow marks—are left on the world somewhere or other. Since counterflow marks are exactly those that cannot or would not be produced by nature, counterflow is inescapably linked to gaps in the normal causal flow of nature. For instance, there is a substantial gap between the potential results of any and all unaided processes in nature and the existence of a diesel bulldozer—a gap that, when confronted by a diesel bulldozer, we bridge by appeal to human agency. Similarly there is a gap between what nature would or could do and the existence of a Martian stainless steel Stonehenge replica—a gap our explanations would bridge by appeal to the activity of aliens. We might call such inference to alien activity an *alien-of-the-gaps* argument. Gap-based inferences are foundational to our identification of artifacts as products of agent activity and in the case of human and alien activity are unproblematically legitimate. If there is something nature could not or would not produce unaided, yet there it is right in front of us, it follows that something else—a human, alien, or other agent—was involved in its production.

Recognizing Finite Designedness

Our recognition of finite designedness (design by finite agents) typically begins with a recognition of artifactuality, itself in turn based upon recognition of counterflow marks. Sometimes those marks are visible in the end product. For instance, we can identify a diesel bulldozer as a product of agent activity and design simply by examining the bulldozer itself. Sometimes such marks are completely absent from the end product, and identification of artifactuality and designedness can only be made from examination of the production processes. For instance, it might be impossible to determine that some molecule of some familiar protein has been synthesized merely from an examination of that molecule itself. That it had been artificially synthesized could, however, be determined if one could investigate the process of its production—that process involving all sorts of designed artifactuality, including labs, glassware and so forth.

In some cases, neither the end product nor even the processes once underway might reveal intentional, counterflow activity, but the initial conditions triggering the process out of which the end product is produced might be enormously and obviously artificial. Suppose that two mice (male and female) were produced by cloning and that they subsequently produced a litter in the usual mouse manner. Examination of the mice in that litter or of the processes of their conception and birth would not reveal anything out of the ordinary. Yet had it not been for the substantial, intentional intervention of human scientists involved in bringing about key necessary conditions for the eventual existence of that litter (i.e., the initial cloning of the parents), the litter would never have existed. Agent counterflow activity was crucially and obviously involved in the initial conditions.

In these and most other cases recognition of counterflow and artifactuality is the starting point toward recognition that something is designed. In some cases we may be able even to identify specifically what the design is. Sometimes the agents producing an artifact have had some particular purpose in producing it, and we are able to tell what that purpose was from investigation of the artifact. Archaeology provides various examples. Alien signals might provide possible cases as well. In the *Contact* binary prime case, we could identify the thinking manifested in the pattern. Or we might be able to determine that the artifact has a key role in the production or preservation of some *value.*

In other cases while we might be unable to discover what the purpose actually was, we might nonetheless be able to tell that there *was* some purpose or other and that the artifact in question was indeed intentionally generated. How might we tell that?

There are a variety of possible clues here. Suppose that (via, for example, counterflow marks) we know that we are dealing with an artifact—that the activity of some agent was involved in its production. If that artifact is enormously complex, or if we establish that its production would have taken significant care, attention or resources, then the conclusion that it is designed—whatever that design might actually be—is certainly a reasonable one. And we do as a matter of fact make such judgements. The Smithsonian reportedly has an entire collection of artifacts, obviously produced with some intention in mind, but the purposes of which have been completely lost. Still, we recognize that they were designed. Similarly if on first arriving upon Mars we came upon some wildly complex alien artifact or one that had clearly required enormous care and commitment of resources to produce, we would likely not put it into the "idly whittled-stick" category of alien artifact but would—probably correctly—conclude that it was intentionally produced and designed, even if we had no clue what it was for and even if we did not have the relevant (alien) concepts for properly describing it.

Of course, there is no guarantee that we can always identify design, always recognize designedness or always recognize artifactuality and counterflow. It is possible that we might confront cases where we were unable to tell whether we were dealing with a genuine artifact or some unusual natural phenomenon. Archaeologists trying to separate extremely primitive hand axes from stones chipped and formed by natural processes are frequently in that situation. Indeed, if there are technologically advanced aliens in our part of the cosmos, we might come upon things that are actually alien artifacts but that we mistakenly think are purely natural. There are a number of scientists who believe that life is not native to the earth and that the organisms we see around us descended from ancestors deliberately produced and transported here by advanced alien races. Were that true, then things we take to be completely natural—essentially everything that lives on earth—would actually be results of deliberate alien activity and design.[5]

Supernatural Design

The general conceptual structure outlined above would apply fairly well to some instances of design produced by supernatural agents as well. It is in principle possible for a supernatural being to bring about virtually any artifact that we humans (or aliens) can. In such cases the phenomenon produced would be as identifiably artifactual and designed (and on exactly the same evidence) as it would be were humans to have produced it. Of course, examining such an object might not tell us that the agent in question was supernatural—just as examining some unusual artifact on earth might not tell us whether it had been produced by humans or produced by covert aliens engaged in a counterfeit earth-souvenir ring for the market back home on Mars. In fact, in the supernatural case it might be that we could not even in principle discover that the agent in question was supernatural. Or perhaps we could never in principle have adequate evidence to conclude that the agent was supernatural. Or perhaps even if we could legitimately arrive at such conclusions, it might still be illegitimate to acknowledge it within a scientific context.[6] But whether or not any of those positions is correct, they are irrelevant to the possibility of our properly identifying the object in question as designed. Even had the Martian stainless steel Stonehenge replica been created by a supernatural agent, any human survey team that managed to overlook the fact that the object was designed would be inept indeed.

Counterflow means. A supernatural being would be able to employ a much wider range of means than would humans or other finite creatures (e.g., aliens). A supernatural being could, of course, employ exactly the same means and methods that we do in bringing about, say, a watch—could construct a factory employing the same principles we do, with the relevant sorts of machinery to form and assemble the parts. Of course, a supernatural agent might know of alternative (yet perfectly natural) means, employing principles of which we were unaware, or that we could not understand, or that we were for numerous reasons unable to employ. Or a supernatural agent might make a watch indistinguishable from some human watch by means involving breaking or suspending laws of nature. Or a supernatural being might simply create such a watch *ex nihilo.*

Precosmic initial conditions. The above different types of supernatural activity would all involve supernatural agent intervention into the course of history and would, like human activity, leave counterflow marks (whether we could recognize them—or even see them—or not). There is, however, one means available *only* to a supernatural *creating* agent and one involving no intervention in the course of nature at all.[7] A supernatural agent who *created* a cosmos could build design into the very structure and interrelationships among the fundamental laws governing that cosmos and/or into the created, initial empirical conditions of that cosmos upon which the created laws were to operate. In fact, those laws and conditions could be deliberately structured so that those laws operating upon those conditions would result in preselected and intended patterns, phenomena or creatures being exemplified billions of years later. That is at least a *possibility* for such an agent. And it seems clear that any such eventuality would exemplify *design.*

But some unique aspects of designedness emerge here. In the above case since the results in question would arise from natural law operating upon ultimate, primordial initial conditions, no *further* specific supernatural action would be required. There would need be no *intervention* anywhere into cosmic causal history, there would be no gaps in nature, and the emergence of specific instances of design billions of years later would not involve any *counterflow* at all. So if a supernatural agent indirectly constructed life, for example, we could scientifically investigate the origin of life without seeing direct supernatural agent activity, seeing only the operating of natural laws and conditions constructing life.

Furthermore, part of creating a cosmos is choosing the laws and conditions of that cosmos—in other words, *specifying what nature itself will be.* Prior to the initial creating activity there simply would be no complete *nature* for anything to run counter to, and consequently there would be no counterflow either in the primordial initial conditions of the cosmos, nor in the selected laws themselves.

Those facts have two consequences for recognition of such designs. First, recall that recognition of designedness typically involves recognition of artifactuality that in turn rests upon recognition of counterflow. But in the present cases there will be no counterflow to provide that foundation. So what will recognition of design *in nature* rest upon? The usual answers are complexity of various sorts, improbability of various degrees, production paths of a certain precariousness, specific sorts of adaptation of means to ends and so on.

But the status of those answers is complicated by a second consequence. Some things function best as clues to designedness in the context of identifiable artifactuality (that identifiability again resting typically upon counterflow). For instance, if we know that something is an artifact, then if that artifact is tremendously complex we generally conclude that it was designed (or at least that it was intentionally made as it is). We typically do *not* think that such tremendous complexity was just an accidental result of "inattentive whittling."

But just bare complexity or bare high improbability seem not to have the same degree of evidential force. That you should be wearing just the ring you have on, containing specific atoms of some metal produced in the supernova of precisely the star that did it, occurring at just the right time and place and traveling on just the right path to end up in just the right place to be found by just the right miner to end up in just the right ring in just the right store for just the right person to buy for you—is *wildly* improbable. But it evidently happened. Yet we do not typically take that wild improbability alone as grounds for thinking that the entire sequence was *designed.*

The point is that a variety of factors, which *in the context of artifactuality* do seem to constitute evidence of design, do not seem *by themselves* to constitute evidence that is nearly as powerful. So the second consequence is this: reliance upon such factors in arguments for design in nature or upon analogical arguments based upon parallels to known human artifacts, may be a bit riskier than usually appreciated. The complexity *of an artifact* may indeed suggest design, but mere complexity alone may not. That is not to say that there is no evidence or no good argument for design in nature but only that the situation may be less straightforward than sometimes assumed.

Design and Science

It is widely held that the concept of supernatural design is illegitimate in science—that it must be barred from both scientific descriptions and scientific explanations. Those who advocate such prohibitions typically do not mean to ban the basic concept of design itself from science—only the concept of supernatural design.

Finite design and science. There is, as most such prohibitionists see it, absolutely nothing wrong with reference to *finite* design—whether human, alien or whatever—within science, because such design involves only beings which are in one very broad sense *natural.*[8] Archeology attempts to discover, identify and explain designedness and even specific design. The SETI program is aimed at discovering, identifying and understanding designed electromagnetic artifacts produced by aliens. And no one would object in principle to the identification by human explorers on other planets of some phenomenon as either artifact or designed by aliens.

It is even possible that we might—quite properly and scientifically—come to the conclusion that some things we had previously thought to be purely natural were actually results of alien design activity. For instance, as noted earlier, a few secular scientists have come to believe that life could not have originated on earth by natural processes and have concluded that life was deliberately designed and then seeded here by aliens.[9] Those scientists might be spectacularly wrong, but the view itself is not inherently unscientific. There is simply no a priori reason for thinking that science must conclude that life originated here on earth rather than somewhere else. Nor is there any a priori reason for thinking that if life did not originate here, science simply could never discover that truth on the basis of (among other things) revealing characteristics of living organisms on earth.

But if such a conclusion could even in principle be legitimately scientific and could be discovered from empirical investigation of organisms, then it follows that it is at least *in principle* possible that the organisms around us should carry evidences of having been designed. In any case, appeal to design produced by finite agents is perfectly legitimate in scientific contexts. Furthermore, there is nothing inherently unscientific even in claiming to identify evidences of design in living organisms (or in other phenomena within the "natural" realm). So if there are difficulties with the idea of genuinely scientific evidences of supernatural design in nature, the difficulties are rooted in the *supernatural* part of that equation. What might such difficulties be?

Supernatural design and science. It is important to distinguish between the possibility of identifying as designed something *that was in fact* (perhaps unknown to us) designed by a supernatural agent and the possibility of identifying something as having been designed by a supernatural agent. Suppose that our Martian stainless steel Stonehenge replica had been designed by a supernatural agent. We might not know that a supernatural agent had designed it. We might be completely unable to determine *that* fact, but there would be no serious question about the basic fact of its being designed. A Mars survey team would not be violating any canons of science in taking it to be designed. Anyone attempting to give a fully scientific explanation of that replica would not commit a scientific mistake in taking its designedness into account. Again that would be true even if the (unknown) fact of the matter was that a supernatural agent had designed it, made it, and placed it there. This indicates that any plausible prohibition on supernatural design within science cannot bar recognition and admission of the basic fact of designedness—no matter what the source. In other words, the identity of the designer need not be of crucial relevance to the proper identifiability of design.

Recall the earlier conclusion that there was no bar in principle to scientific recognition of any evidences of design even in what we would ordinarily identify as natural phenomena. We have just seen that there are no good grounds in principle for barring recognition of evidences of design even if the (perhaps unknown) fact of the matter is that the design is supernatural. Together, those suggest that *if nature or various things in nature are in fact designed, science cannot be forbidden to recognize that designedness even should the ultimate truth of the matter be that it was a supernatural being that did the designing.*

Some design prohibitionists might even accept that. So exactly what is the usual prohibition a prohibition *of?* The only prohibition even potentially plausible would be against recognizing (or claiming to recognize) within the scientific context *that the design is supernatu-*

ral. What might be the grounds for that restriction?

Methodological Naturalism

The standard prohibition on the supernatural in science is generally referred to as *methodological naturalism.* The basic idea is that science must proceed as if philosophical naturalism is true (whether or not it is)—making no reference to supernatural design, causation or activity in its formal scientific descriptions, explanations and theories.[10]

Methodological naturalism is widely accepted—even by many Christians within science.[11] There are, I think, five primary reasons for that wide acceptance. They are (1) the belief that methodological naturalism is demanded by the very definition of *science,* (2) the belief that theories concerning the supernatural can have no stable, empirically testable contents, (3) the belief that such theories have historically been complete scientific failures, (4) the belief that all such theories are versions of "God-of-the-gaps" theories and that such theories are scientifically unacceptable and (5) the belief that permitting use of design theories would erode science by fostering scientific laziness. None of those reasons, it seems to me, fares well under scrutiny. We will look very briefly at each in turn.

1. Definitions. The issue of what is or is not demanded in (or excluded from) science "by definition" is much less clear than it seemed prior to Kuhn. One of the lessons of Kuhn, recall, is that a variety of *metaphysical commitments* are utterly indispensable to science itself. Establishing a definitional prohibition against supernatural design would thus require determining what sorts of "metaphysical" principles are or are not permissible in science, then showing that supernatural design falls on the wrong side of that boundary. That is vastly more difficult than merely emphatically pointing out that supernatural design involves the supernatural.

One factor making this definitional approach difficult is that, as we saw earlier in the book, there is no universally accepted *formal* definition of *science,* and proposed definitions almost invariably run into nasty difficulties sooner or later. That makes reliance upon a definition of science a bit "iffy." Furthermore, if we turn to some of the *informal* definitions suggested by scientists themselves, we find small comfort for prohibitionists. One such definition is that science is an attempt to get at the truth *no holds barred*. That is not likely to provide support for attempts to bar particular concepts. The scientific attitude has usually been characterized as a commitment to following the evidence wherever it leads. That does not look like promising ammunition for someone pushing an official policy of refusing to allow science to follow evidence to supernatural design no matter what the evidence turns out to be. Science has often been described as organized and formalized common sense. There might be some question about what actually constitutes common sense, but I suspect that most humans at most times in most cultures have considered it just good common sense that there is a supernatural realm and that supernatural activity is deeply linked to the structure, governance and history of the cosmos. Not much help for prohibitionists here either.

Some—especially some Christians—have argued that while there is indeed a supernatural realm that may impinge upon the natural realm, the natural realm has its own integral identity, character and operative principles, and the task of science is to trace the fabric of those natural structures in and on their own terms. There may be interventions (e.g., scriptural miracles), and such interventions may be of utterly crucial significance. But, it is argued, they have no bearing upon the character of the natural—which by this definition is what the created order would do and be in the absence of such interventions. Since the latter is the focus of science, science should properly proceed as if there were no interventions—at least, it should not formally take account of them.[12]

That may be a perfectly defensible position, but it certainly removes some of the starch from the claim that something is or is not scientific. It commits science to either having to deliberately ignore major (possibly even *observable*) features of the material realm or having to refrain from even considering the obvious and only workable explanation, should it turn out that those features clearly resulted from supernatural activity. Further, recall discussion from an earlier chapter indicating that any imposed policy of naturalism in science has the potential not only of eroding any self-correcting capability of science but of preventing science from reaching certain truths. Any imposed policy of methodological naturalism will have precisely the same potential consequences.

2. Empirical emptiness. It might be argued that although there may be no complete definition of *science,* we do know at least some of the essential components of any such definition. Among them is the requirement that any legitimately scientific theory or concept have some specifiable empirical content—that it have empirical implications, be empirically testable, empirically falsifiable and so forth. The problem with *supernatural design,* this line of thought continues, is that it has no stable empirical content. Indeed, it can be adapted to essentially anything in nature, or if the adaptation proves difficult it can simply be claimed that there really is some design or other, but that we just have not yet grasped it. But, the objection continues, in the face of such hyperflexibility the alleged empirical content of the concept simply evaporates.

That objection is not a frivolous one, and it does have some force. But two serious reservations are worth noting. First, recall from earlier discussion that no theory *just by itself* generates any empirical predictions or consequences at all. Theories predict only in conjunction with a variety of other things—bridge principles, initial conditions and so forth. And it is possible that the idea of supernatural design could, in conjunction with other principles, have empirical implications.[13]

The second reservation is that different parts of science operate in different ways, on different levels and must answer to different demands. Consider the principle of the uniformity of nature. Historically the underpinning of that principle is philosophical. It is not empirically testable—indeed, what test results might *mean* is itself determined in part in a context already defined by that very principle. The principle of uniformity is not at empirical risk—no matter what results are produced by what experiment, we would not decide that nature must have just changed the rules and abandon the principle of uniformity. Indeed, we *protect* that principle, typically not even considering alternatives to it. Should what we took to be a uniformity begin to break down, we would simply conclude that we had misidentified what the *real* uniformity was. The principle of uniformity by itself makes no empirical predictions. It is involved in predictions only when we have specified some *respect* in which we take nature to be uniform. Otherwise, it says nothing whatever. It is unlimitedly flexible—no matter what turns up, we take uniformity to be consistent with it and able to accommodate it.

So uniformity makes no predictions, is untestable, is not at empirical risk, can be bent to accommodate anything, is preferentially protected and rests ultimately upon philosophical considerations. Yet the uniformity principle is not only legitimately scientific, it is utterly essential to science. Demands that it have evident empirical content, be testable, make predictions and so forth, are inappropriate to the type of principle it is, operating at the level in science on which it functions. But that suggests the possibility that depending upon how and where it operates in science, *supernatural design* might properly be no more subject to those demands than is the principle of uniformity. At the very least, since the charges leveled against *supernatural design* typically involve characteristics displayed by other perfectly legitimate concepts within science (e.g., uniformity), the conclusion that the mere having of those characteristics disqualifies *supernatural design* from science will require some additional—and perhaps difficult—work.

If either of the above two objections (definitions and empirical emptiness) were compelling, there would be difficulties *in principle* for introducing the idea of supernatural design into science. But objections have also been based upon more practical, pragmatic considerations. Let us look briefly at the three primary objections of that sort.

3. Historical track record. The claim here is that while *supernatural design* may not in principle be illegitimate in scientific contexts, it has been tried historically and has simply failed. Geocentric theories do not violate any normative principles of good scientific procedure and may have been scientifically useful in their time. But it would be extremely silly to try resuscitating them now. Similarly, it is argued, design theories might not violate any normative scientific principles, but they had their chance, ultimately failed, and it would be a waste of valuable scientific time and effort to turn back the clock and take them seriously again.

But plausible as that sounds, it is not just obvious that the concept of supernatural design was a historical failure. It has been often noted by historians of science that various theological themes (including specifically the doctrine of creation with its fundamental implications of design) played important roles in the rise and early career of modern science. In fact, some historians have argued that modern science as we know it would not have arisen as it did without that formative theological context. This suggests the possibility that concepts like the designedness of nature were essential to science's beginnings and may have generated some of the ongoing conceptual shapes of science that we, having forgotten their origins, now take as basic givens of the scientific outlook.

Of course, it might be argued that such concepts were both legitimate and even scientifically useful in getting science up and running but have long outlived any such usefulness. As an analogy, consider the construction of an arch in a medieval cathedral. While a wooden scaffolding might be essential for constructing such an arch, once the capstone is in place the scaffold is not only no longer needed but now constitutes an obstacle to those wishing to go through the arch. But the present case may not be quite so simple. In fact, some of the weightbearing members of science may still be remnants of early design concepts. Indeed, the physicist Paul Davies once remarked that "Science began as an outgrowth of theology, and all scientists, whether atheists or theists . . . accept an essentially theological worldview."[14] It may be that we sometimes do not see the empirical ramifications of design simply because science as we now learn it is already immersed in empirical consequences of design that are parts of its very fabric. As Einstein once asked: What does a fish know of the water in which it swims all its life?

4. *God of the gaps.* Suppose that we come across some phenomenon for which we are unable to find a good, natural explanation. Were it scientifically permissible, there might be a strong temptation in such situations to conclude that there just *is not* any natural explanation—that the phenomenon in question has resulted from supernatural activity. Theories appealing to supernatural activity to account for various phenomena in nature are frequently termed *God-of-the-gaps*

theories and are typically viewed as desperate, scientifically bogus attempts to cover our scientific ignorance with the appearance of an explanation. Such theories are generally seen as historically unfortunate for the cause of religion since, it is claimed, the gaps of ignorance in which such theories flourish have a tendency to disappear as science advances, leaving religion with little more in the scientific realm than a long, misguided trail of failure littered with shattered theories.

It is nearly unanimously charged that design theories are simply *God-of-the-gaps* theories and that such theories are automatically defective. Popular as that picture is, it is substantially skewed. First, *design* theories need not involve gaps at all. Suppose that a meteor swarm hit the moon, and after the dust settled it was discovered that the impacts had left thousands of small, uniformly sized meteor craters arranged in such a way that they constituted a really nifty proof of a previously unknown mathematical theorem that held the key to solving a bunch of global problems. Few would doubt that this episode exhibited design.

Suppose further that we fired up our new time machine, traced back the history of the meteor swarm and every individual meteor in it, and discovered that absolutely everything in that history back to the big bang was absolutely and completely natural—there were no gaps anywhere in the causal history of the entire sequence. We would not, I think, abandon our previous design conclusion—we would simply conclude that the design had been deliberately structured into the initiating event of the cosmos itself.

What our story indicates is that design and gaps are not necessarily linked and that the charge that design cases must of necessity be gap cases is mistaken. A *gap* has to do with the causal *history* of a phenomenon. *Design* has to do with whether or not the phenomenon has characteristics (however produced, whatever the immediate means of production) exemplifying a specific type of agent-dependent, mind-resonating pattern. Thus to claim that any design theory has to be a gap theory is simply to confuse two quite distinct issues.

Second, *many historical design theories did not involve gaps.* Some of the more popular design theories in the early nineteenth century were based upon the structure, inter-relationships and dovetailing of the basic laws of nature—not on gaps in nature's capabilities that required supernatural bridging.[15] It was widely held among design advocates—and can be found explicitly in the writings of, for example, Bacon and Boyle—that the deliberate achieving of some intended result through indirect means (involving the structure of laws and the initial conditions of the creation itself) demonstrated more impressive wisdom, foresight and planning than did activity within cosmic causal history—interventions to bridge gaps.[16] This was a common theme in the writing of Christian scientists. Thus the claim that design theories historically were all gap theories is simply inaccurate.[17]

Third, as noted earlier, whatever its other defects, *gap cases* are at least *logically unproblematic.* If nature and chance cannot produce some phenomenon, yet there it inarguably is in front of us, it follows that something else did produce it—and agents of various sorts are essentially the only other alternative. And if we have good grounds for thinking that neither humans nor other finite creatures have the relevant capability, then supernatural agency is the only option left. Of course, those things may be difficult to *establish,* but that is irrelevant to the logical point.

Fourth, some design cases even involving gaps were *not based upon frustrated ignorance.* Our own postulation of a diesel-bulldozer gap is not driven by ignorance but by genuine knowledge of limitations on nature's capabilities. Similarly, historical design conclusions were often based upon characteristics that had a particularly mind-resonant character and that were taken to be positive evidences of designedness because of that special character independent of any considerations of exactly how the characteristics were produced.[18]

5. Scientific laziness. Beginning at least as far back as the early seventeenth century and continuing to the present, some thinkers have expressed the fear that if supernatural explanations were allowed in science, then scientists would be tempted to appeal to supernatural activity as the explanation in scientifically difficult cases and might thus abandon too quickly scientific searches that otherwise might eventually turn up a correct, natural explanation. That is a legitimate concern, and it does provide a legitimate cautionary note.[19] But the fact that scientists might be tempted to adopt such theories too easily surely does not by itself imply that such theories should be forever placed off limits no matter what evidence might turn up. Some theorizers might too easily leap to alien explanations (for lights in the sky, crop circles, stalled cars, etc.). But that tendency would hardly justify a refusal even to consider explanatory reference to aliens if the first humans on Mars really did find a stainless steel replica of Stonehenge. So while care is called for, under some circumstances such a prohibition may screen science from seeing truth. That would not seem to be the most productive form of care.[20]

Norms and Strategies

In light of the above it is not at all obvious that we have some rational or scientific obligation to adopt methodological naturalism in science. In fact, even were such justifications correct the last three would support at most the adoption of methodological naturalism as merely a pragmatic strategy. As a first approach to scientific problems, methodological naturalism may be a valuable—even the best—strategy. A search for natural explanations may virtually always be the best place to start. But if it becomes clear that limiting the search in that way hinders *understanding* of nature, if there are things in nature that constitute the natural equivalent of the stainless steel Stonehenge replica on Mars, then that limitation itself needs examination. And such examination is perfectly legitimate. However useful in practice, a pragmatically justified strategy does not constitute a norm that is inviolable no matter what the evidence.

The Intelligent Design Movement

As noted earlier, theories asserting the designedness of nature (or of various things in nature) have become increasingly prominent in the past few years. Suspicions that there was something about the fundamental structure of the cosmos that might require extraordinary explanation first surfaced seriously in physics around a quarter of a century ago and involved a cluster of issues including *anthropic cosmological* principles and *fine-tuning* arguments. Some of the proposed explanations were relatively tame, some involved design, and some were *really* extraordinary.[21]

More recently a number of (primarily) Christians in various disciplines have formed a loose coalition known as the *intelligent design* (or ID) movement. The ID movement exhibits a fair amount of diversity, but the center of gravity of the group is a rejection of methodological naturalism, at least as any sort of *norm*.[22] The fundamental contentions of the group are that design concepts can be given genuinely empirical content, cannot be ruled out of science *a priori* and that theories of design in nature should be given a fair scientific chance.[23] To charges that design theories were already given that chance historically and failed, design advocates respond that the evidential situation is now very different, that design theories can now be given much more sophisticated construction and content, and that design theories can be explanatorily competitive, especially in light of the extraordinary complexity and structures being uncovered in, for example, biochemistry.[24]

The design evidences cited by this group generally consist of either particular types of complexity, certain types of improbability in certain defined circumstances or considerations involving "information" in biological systems.[25] Given that design and gaps are separable issues, the evidences proposed as marks of design do not necessarily have to be linked to gaps. (In fact, even some of the more prominent design advocates have no serious quarrel with the possibility that all forms of life are descended from a common ancestor.) The majority of those within the movement, however, believe that there are gaps in nature, that the existence of various gaps can be *scientifically* substantiated and that evolution cannot close all such gaps. (That combination of views of course points to the occurrence of supernatural interventions in nature historically.)

Although the bulk of the ID movement rejects large-scale (macro) evolution, a few do accept some type of macroevolutionary history of life on earth. And some who reject macroevolution nonetheless admit that they could be wrong—that some form of macroevolution could turn out to be correct. However, given the biochemical and empirical evidence as they see it, nearly all within the ID movement take the odds of that to be quite small and would insist that even were some form of macroevolution correct, a *Darwinian* (chance-driven) evolution was empirically hopelessly inadequate. But even if life had an evolutionary history, that would not, on their view, change the fact that the biological realm exhibited evidences of deliberate design.[26]

There are other differences of opinion within the movement, but the general contention is that prohibitions on considering deliberate design as a scientific explanation of some aspects of nature are not legitimate and that a number of recent scientific discoveries may be best—or even only—made intelligible by reference to design.

Conclusion

What should we make of all this? If the foregoing is correct, there are no compelling grounds for ironclad prohibitions against genuinely scientific design theories, should any such theories arise.

Are there present prospects of such? Most people within the design movement believe that the answer is a clear yes, and most critics of the movement give an unequivocal no. Among factors underlying that disagreement there is on the one side a tendency to overestimate purely natural science and on the other side a tendency to underestimate nature. Overestimating science disposes one toward a belief that regardless of what explanatory puzzles confront us at the moment, human science unaided by any concepts beyond the purely natural, will ultimately conquer. Such a position could obviously induce scientists to pursue naturalistic hopes to unreasonable and even scientifically counterproductive lengths. At the other pole, underestimating nature may incline one to see gaps too readily and to not appreciate the enormous, remarkable capabilities nature in fact has.[27]

Ultimately, of course, scientists themselves will have the most say on this issue, but my own view is that for the moment the question is genuinely open. We are not in a position to say definitively that design concepts offer nothing that science will ever need or will ever find genuinely useful in its attempts to make sense of what we may discover within the cosmos. And nothing guarantees that we will never uncover a gap in nature itself that sober, rigorous scientific assessment will identify as being bridgeable only via agent activity. It is even possible that such a moment has already arrived. Contrary to some secular propaganda, there are fairly long stretches of empty space between any explicit chemical processes whose details we know and the structure of even simple forms of life. Unaided nature may be unable to navigate those stretches.[28] There may already be secular biologists who at around 3 a.m. find themselves just a *bit* anxious about the presumed natural origin of life or about electric rotary *E. coli* motors or about the fine-tuning of the cosmos.

On the other hand, it does not seem to me that our grasp of nature's capabilities is thorough enough and broad enough to permit us to simply dismiss the possibility of discovering that (perhaps presently unknown) natural processes can bridge what at the moment look, even to our best science, like gaps. We *may* be approaching such a moment in developments in, for example, "complexity theory."[29] Of course, given that evidences of design can be completely independent of gaps, it would still be possible to argue that specific phenomena exhibited evidences of design resulting from processes that, while natural, were themselves intentionally structured to produce just such design. But in that case, the cited phenomena would have to constitute evidence of design in and of themselves. Although they may be suggestive, some of the currently popular design evidences do not strike me as settling the issue *scientifically.*

We must be a bit cautious about underestimating nature's capabilities. During its history science has been surprised by nature pretty regularly, and it may happen again. And we must be equally wary of overestimating science—particularly our own. During its history science has often been overestimated in various circles, and that is almost certain to happen again.

There are some parts of nature that when experienced uncritically seem to generate in us a deep sense of their createdness and design. Kant spoke of the "starry skies above" as affecting us like that, and Psalm 19:1 speaks of the heavens declaring God's glory. Furthermore, there are things in nature that even when (perhaps especially when) viewed *critically,* generate a nearly irresistible intuition of designedness. We find such things both in general structures in nature (e.g., cosmic fine-tuning) and in specifics (e.g., *E. coli* motors). I think that it is in principle possible for defensible design cases to be made, and such cases need not violate any fundamental requirements or conditions of science. But whatever the fate of *formal scientific* arguments in this area, we are violating no broad principles of *rationality* in thinking of the creation around us—perhaps inescapably—in terms of supernatural design.

9

Christianity &
Scientific Pursuits

We *concluded earlier that Christians need not fear science.*
But that leaves open questions of whether science is a legitimate pursuit for Christians, whether it has special worth to Christians, whether Christians have special reasons for pursuing it and whether Christian belief might have contribution to make to the general scientific project. It is to such questions we now turn.

The Legitimacy of Science
Although many Christians have unhesitatingly accepted and practiced science, and many of the best-known scientists historically have been Christians, others have felt that science was not a legitimate pursuit for Christians. What has been behind that rejection?

First, some Christians have argued that we are not to be concerned with the things of this world and that other things related to the central tasks of Christianity—witnessing, for instance—are more important.

Spreading the gospel is indeed crucial, and if Christians had to choose between that and doing science, science would have to take a back seat. But the choice is not an either/or choice for the Christian community as a whole and not always even for individuals. The Christian life is the whole life, the abundant life, and it has room for fishermen, physicians, tentmakers, tax gatherers—and scientists.

Second, some Christians have felt that science was, perhaps inherently, contrary to Christianity. After all, does not science assume determinism (relieving us of moral responsibility) and strict uniformity (denying that God can act miraculously in the world)? Isn't it science that we have to thank for theories like evolution and the big bang, and don't they violate Scripture? We will discuss the relationship of science to Christian belief and to Scripture in more detail in the next chapter, but two observations are in order here. First, it is often the rigid generalizing of the (supposed) presuppositions of science into sweeping worldviews (like positivism) that causes problems rather than their proper and restricted use within science itself. Second, even if science sometimes produces individual theories that look contrary to Scripture, condemning the whole project of science might be like condemning the general enterprise of cooking because occasionally people are poisoned by improperly cooked food. Bad cooking does not make cooking bad. In both cases we might more properly condemn faulty technique than the entire project.

Third, some Christians have seen science as prying where we have no business, trying to *discover* hidden things. But Proverbs 25:2 tells us that "it is the glory of God to conceal a matter; to search out a matter is the glory of kings." It is the *glory* of *kings* to search out a matter. That does not sound as though trying to discover the hidden is to be seen as improper.

Reasons for Doing Science

Just because something is permissible does not mean that there are good reasons for actually doing it. Are there, for the Christian, good reasons for doing science? Does science have any distinctive value and worth for the Christian?

Many Christians have said yes, and a variety of justifications have been offered for that answer. For instance, God gave to us the task of caring for and tending our part of his creation.[1] But responsible stewardship requires knowledge of how the things in our keeping work, knowledge concerning the proper care of and best use of the things we have been placed over. Science can be a vehicle for acquiring such knowledge.

Further, many Christians believe that God's command to subdue the earth[2] is still in force (others believe that it no longer applies after the Fall). Subduing the earth also requires knowledge, providing again a role for science.

Many Christians believe that God created us as *knowing* beings. Humans do always seem to want to know and to understand things. We are inveterate theorizers, and science is the most formal channel through which that side of our natures can be expressed with respect to the workings of nature.

Somewhat more theological reasons have been offered also. For instance, nature is God's creation, and many Christians have seen nature as revealing God. By studying nature they expect to learn not only what God did in creating but about God himself. Nature is sometimes referred to as a book of revelation, and it is through science that we learn to read that book.[3] Some Christians believe that doing science, making new discoveries, exploring the intricacies of nature and coming to appreciate the details of creation are all ways of glorifying God. God judged his creation good.[4] That fact alone is mandate enough for some to pursue knowing his good creation.

Finally, we have been explicitly instructed to help the sick, the hungry and the poor. Surely we are in a better position to help in such cases by virtue of knowing the causes of disease, the proper treatment of illness, how to produce better crops and so on. Science can help us in doing the tasks we have been given.

Of course, science has played an equally prominent role in the destruction in which we humans perennially engage. Historically, military demands have been a major driving force behind various sorts of research as well as a source of a great deal of the financial support for science and scientists. So also have greed (in some corporate scientific research), a desire to escape the consequences of one's actions (for instance, some research into techniques for abortion) and a variety of other not-so-pretty motivations.

Thus although science seems to be a permissible pursuit for the Christian, and although there are distinctive reasons a Christian might have for doing science, and although science and its results can have special value for the Christian, Christians in science are still under deep obligation to look to their particular reasons for doing science. They must consider the potential for harm and rebellion against God their particular work might have, and they must work to make their efforts in science fit into the larger pattern of their obedience to God. Outside such a context, the work of a scientists—even of one who claims allegiance to Christ—can be disastrous on a variety of scales.

Christianity and the Foundations of Science

As we saw earlier, justification for the foundational presuppositions of science cannot be provided wholly by science itself. It must come at least partially from outside science. Where might such justification come from?

In chapter one we mentioned the Christian context as a justification of the general character of science. A number of authors have argued that belief in a personal Creator was, if not a prerequisite for the rise of modern science, at least an enormous aid to that rise. Although other cultures boasted longer histories and technological traditions, it was in Western Europe with its strong Christian tradition that modern science emerged.

Some ancient Greeks tended to view the material world as not worthy of study. In other ancient pagan cultures nature was seen as deity, which made poking at it (experimentally or empirically) inappropriate or even hazardous. Many Eastern cultures saw reality as ruled by rigid necessities, making empirical investigation superfluous. Others saw chance or chaos as the ruling principle, making investigation of nature pointless and inevitably unsuccessful.

But Christians saw the world as a creation (thus orderly and uniform) of a Person (thus rational) who had created freely (thus requiring empirical investigation) unconstrained by our prejudices and expectations (thus requiring open-minded investigation). So the basic character of science grew to be what one could expect from a Christian outlook. That is not to say that one could deduce the basic outlines of a scientific method from Christianity but that those outlines fit well with Christian doctrine. And besides the more general themes, there are more specific characteristics and presuppositions of science that Christianity either anticipates or provides justification for.

It is generally presupposed within science that an objective, independent reality exists outside of and beyond us which science studies (contrary to various forms of both idealism and relativism). That is exactly what one would expect if the nature science studies were a creation. *God* created it independently of us, according to his plan and without our concurrence or consent.

Another key presupposition is that of the uniformity which underlies the belief in nature's predictability and which also provides support for the usual requirement that scientific results be reproducible. But Scripture tells us of God's faithfulness in the governance of the cosmos. Uniformity is what we would expect of a creation that is established by a God who is faithful and that is governed by his edicts.

It is a further assumption of science that nature is comprehendible, that we can understand it. That is what we might expect, given that God created with wisdom and that the reason by which we try to understand the creation was created by the same God.

Epistemic Values

As we saw earlier, epistemic values have recently come to be seen as crucial to theories of scientific rationality. There is Christian justification for some of the shape of emerging conceptions of scientific rationality.

Many of the specific epistemic values discussed earlier seem to be different sides of a single intuition—that nature is a *cosmos*. Thus we anticipate that theories speaking of patterns instead of coincidences are more likely to be right, and that is the core of the notion of simplicity. We expect that theories speaking of patterns that can cover large stretches of reality instead of restricted patches will more likely be closer to truth, and that is the basic thrust of the breadth-of-scope requirement. We expect theories that reveal new and uncover old but previously hidden patterns, and that point to novel (but correct) manifestations of previous patterns, to be more likely on the right track than those that cannot, and that is the fruitfulness idea. And given that *cosmos* precludes fundamental chaos, we insist on self-consistent theories, and since we expect the patterns to be broad and unified, we expect that theories which are even approximately true will mesh with each other. The Christian has a powerful reason for believing that we live in a cosmos. It is God's creation, which he says reveals his character. So we expect pattern and unity. We expect order and regularity.

The patterns may be deep. We may not understand them all. But we expect them to be there. And we might even find here a justification for some more basic epistemic matters. Why should we rely on our senses, as the empirical foundation demands? Why should we think that our thought patterns exhibit rationality? Why should we think that others have experiences and make inferences similar to our own and which can function as objective, communal checks on our science? An answer to all of those questions for the Christian is that God created us, all of us, as knowing beings, and he created us for this world, to be knowing beings in this world. That does not guarantee our epistemic infallibility, but it certainly gives us a place to stand epistemologically. An epistemological place to stand is something of which most secular epistemologies (perhaps all of them) cannot boast.

Realism

Although Christianity does not force it on us, it does provide some support for realism. God created us with faculties of sense and reason, and it has been held by many Christians that our senses and our reason are appropriate to and congruent with reality, if rightly used. If so, then if we do correctly use our abilities, we can indeed learn truths, even hidden truths about nature.[5]

Without such a connection between our abilities and truth, some sort of antirealism would be difficult to escape. A purely naturalistic evolution, for instance, would not provide us with such a connection. Evolution does not necessarily select for truth of conceptualizations. Survival and fitness depend on having the appropriate characteristics and engaging in appropriate behavior regardless of what one might *think* one is doing. Darwin himself recognized that, and during at least one stage he worried that evolution might undercut justification for believing in the mind's reliability.[6]

Thus it may be that something other than a pure naturalism is needed to justify the realism that predominates in contemporary philosophy of science and that has predominated historically among scientists. God's having created us for this world and having created us as knowing beings certainly gives us a start on such a justification.

Such a justification would provide for the possibility of our getting to theoretical truths. Our fallenness might partially explain why we have no guarantees of reaching such truths.

Attitudes and Behavior

Respect for nature. There are a number of attitudes required to do science properly, and Christianity supports those well. For instance, Christianity fosters the proper respect for nature that good science requires.[7] For the Christian, the world and everything in it belong to God and consequently have to be respected and treated accordingly. It is not ours to abuse. That respect is kept in balance by God's having granted us the use of nature and by God's having revealed to us that it is, after all, a creation. Our respect for it need not (indeed, must not) reach the pitch of worship, an attitude that would effectively bring science to an end.

Moral principles and virtues. There are also moral principles essential to science. If scientists lacked honesty toward their fellow scientists, integrity concerning their work, humility before the results of their investigation, generosity with the information they gain, self-control in the face of frustration, perseverance through experimental failure, patience in times of slow progress and so on, there would be little effective science. But Scripture points to those virtues, offers help in moving toward them and gives them a foundation in God's law and commandments.

We must keep in mind that objectivity in science is protected in part by the communal nature of science. Why is that communal protection necessary at all? One reason is that some of the above virtues are not always honored, and the scientific community needs protection from these breaches. But those failures should not come as any surprise to the Christian familiar with Scripture's clear-eyed view of our state, our inclinations and our tendencies.

Perspective. So Christianity can provide some justification for many aspects of the character of natural science, its methods and its presuppositions. But besides that, Christianity puts science in proper perspective as being valuable but not the ultimate value; as being competent but not all-competent; as being a proper part of human life but not the whole; as being something humans do but not our highest calling; as providing solutions to some problems but not to the most fundamental human problem, alienation from our Creator.

Losing perspective in any of those areas creates a distortion and a denial of simple human facts of life. Losing that last perspective distorts the facts of Life.

10

Christianity &
the Specific Content
of Science
A Typology

W*e have seen that science does not constitute an effective* weapon against Christianity (chapter seven) and that in fact the fundamental characteristics of science fit well with Christianity on a philosophical level (chapter nine). But there is disagreement even among Christians concerning if and to what extent Christianity bears on the specific content and internal workings of science. Without providing specific answers to those questions we will look now at the context and some of the boundaries within which answers to those questions must be given.

First of all, it should be clear that what one believes concerning the integration of one's science and Christianity will be affected by one's conception of science. There are a number of competing conceptions of science, most of which are versions of the three major types we examined in chapters two, three, four and five. Let us briefly review those three.

A Review

First, the traditional view (chapter two) construed science as empirical, objective and rational. By *empirical,* holders of this conception meant that experiential or observation-based data was the primary (or sole) determinant of theory acceptability. By *objective* they meant that data embarrassing to one's theory could not be ignored, that philosophical or religious principles were to have no say in theory adjudication, and that observational data were public, neutral and independent of the observer. By *rational* they meant that theory evaluation and other processes within science were to be governed by logic and that logical inconsistency or tension was always cause for concern and always demanded resolution.

This picture of science leaves little opportunity for religion to influence it. After all, it is the logical manipulation of neutral and independent data that directs the course and content of science, with an explicit proviso that religious and philosophical principles are to have no say whatever. It almost guarantees separation.

The 1960s and 1970s view, on the other hand (see chapter three), when pushed toward the extreme, almost guaranteed a melding of one's science with one's deeper beliefs. On this type of view it was not just empirical data that determined theory acceptability but a variety of paradigm-related considerations. These paradigm-related considerations were not objective in the traditional sense. Up to a point one could simply ignore embarrassing anomalies. Theories were selected in the light of metaphysical and normative principles contained within the paradigm itself. Data were not neutral but were in part determined by and constituted by the paradigm in question. And not only was the course of science not bound to conform to rigorous logic, but it could not. Paradigms were incommensurable. There was no logic that would allow a rigorous adjudication. And if logical tension arose within one's science, it could be tolerated indefinitely until it got to be too annoying—and there were not any rules for when that point was reached.

This sort of view is hospitable to science being influenced by a variety of beliefs and values, including religion. Some have extended the Kuhnian picture into "Weltanschauung" (worldview) conceptions of science, arguing that one's whole worldview (and not just one's scientific paradigms) affects perception, meaning, theory content and theory selection. In that case, influence of one's religion on one's science is nearly inevitable. The Christian and the nonbeliever will be unable to observe the same things, to mean the same things or to believe the same theories.

Finally, we looked at the direction philosophy of science has been moving over the past several years (chapters four and five). Observation-based data are again vitally important, but the connection to theory is by no means rigid and can vary depending on the level of the theory; and the data need not be the only determinant of theory choice. The data in question are colored by background principles, and theory choice is also affected by background principles, but the coloration and influence are neither arbitrary nor of such a scope as to result in incommensurability or relativism. There are rational constraints on theorizing and theory choice (versus arbitrary subjectivism), but neither the constraints nor rationality are rigid or rule-bound.

On this type of picture religious influence internal to science is neither prohibited nor guaranteed, but there is room for such influence, depending on how one fills in some of the specific details.

There are basically three categories of positions concerning the influence of religion on the internal workings of science: that there is no influence, strong influence or partial influence. The last two categories further subdivide with regard to whether the proposed influence is based on the person in question having certain beliefs and commitments or on Scripture. Let us consider the various possibilities.

Science and Religious Beliefs as Independent

Those who have argued that religion has no bearing on science have typically accepted the traditional view of science. One's Christian beliefs, on this view, did not affect perception, theory choice or any other internal aspect of science since those beliefs were not empirical or scientific beliefs but were religious. Religion and science were put into entirely different compartments, so any interaction was out of the question.

It is possible, however, to hold a more contemporary conception and yet to claim a strict separation between religious belief and science. One could admit that there are many inputs into the inner workings of science besides just the empirical but yet deny that any of those additional influences can be from religion.

Separating science from religion seems to some people to offer two benefits. First, religious beliefs would be safe from assault from science; and second, science would be free of any interference from the religious sector. Cases for such separation are generally based either on a postulation of two distinct realms of reality or on some type of complementarity. We will discuss each in turn.

Separate domains. Some claim that science and religion deal with entirely distinct areas, science with the material realm and religion with the spiritual.[1] Since those realms are often perceived as almost completely unconnected (that belief having roots in Descartes and Kant), science and religion are, on this view, not even about the same things. Consequently there is no common ground on which they can even in principle run into each other. Each holds sway in its domain, and peace is guaranteed.

Despite its popularity, that approach does not seem too promising. It is not really clear how the respective realms are to be divided. In fact, religious statements and scientific statements are often about some of the same subjects. For instance, we can make biological statements about trees, but we also have to say that those same trees are creations of God. We can make astronomical statements about the sun, but we have to admit also that God created it for light. We can make scientific statements about humans, but we must also say that those same humans are created in God's image. A strict separation of the items of creation into those wholly subject to science and those wholly subject to religion does not then seem successful.

Complementarity. The second way of achieving separation has been to admit, even to insist, that science and religion often concern the same objects but to claim that they deal with those objects in different categories of description and different types and levels of explanation. Each type of description and explanation may or may not be complete with respect to its own categories, but none can be *absolutely* complete since descriptions within other *complementary* categories are also needed before one has a complete description of the object in question. Even if we could give a *scientifically* complete description of a tree, that description would not yet say all the things true about that tree; we would also have to speak of God's having created trees, of the purpose for trees in God's plan and so forth. On this complementary picture all of these latter truths about trees are truths on the religious level and fall into a different category from truths on the scientific level, even though they are about the same objects. On this view then there are not two separate domains with everything in creation falling into one or the other, but rather there are alternative, complementary ways of *describing* and *explaining* each of the things in creation. Those ways are independent of each other in that they describe (with distinct, characteristic concepts) and explain (with distinct, characteristic explanatory principles) different levels or aspects of reality but are not inconsistent with or contrary to each other.[2]

Strict complementarity. The strict complementarist then claims that since religious and scientific explanations are on different levels and are independent of one another, both can be *complete* on their respective levels.[3] Thus neither religion nor science can invade the other because their concepts, descriptions and explanations are of different logical types. Being on different levels, there will be *no common ground* on which they can come into conflict. On the scientific level of reality, science confronts no religious barriers. Its method has the final say on all matters within that level, and thus religious truths are irrelevant to the content of science. Science cannot, however, go beyond its level, and thus it can throw up no challenges or roadblocks to religious beliefs and explanations.

Similarly theology can proceed confidently in the knowledge that no matter what science says it has no significant consequences for the fundamentals of religious belief, even where science and theology are discussing the same objects. Theological explanations operate wholly on the theological level and have complete sovereignty there. So science can properly view humans as machines, although theology can properly continue to assert that we bear God's image.[4] Humans can be viewed scientifically as determined mechanisms, although we must maintain theologically that we are free and thus morally responsible. In general, every object, process or event in the physical world can be given an adequate scientific explanation, although all such objects, processes and events can and must *also* be described in terms of God's plan, his acting in the world and so forth.

Despite its popularity there are serious difficulties with strict complementarity. We have seen that scientific explanations are never complete explanations. For one thing they always depend on philosophical presuppositions that in turn may have to find their justification in the realm of religious belief. For another, scientific explanations always involve specification of initial conditions. Even if one accepts the view that our universe resulted from fluctuations in a primordial vacuum, one must stipulate some initial conditions concerning that vacuum. Quite clearly, no matter how one tried to get the universe and all subsequent scientific explanations rolling, one must appeal to some initial *physical* conditions *that are not themselves completely scientifically accounted for.* Thus there is a forced choice between either simply taking those initial conditions as brute givens or else of accounting for them in other terms, such as a theological principle of God's having created those initial conditions. Taking the first option makes it a mistake to claim that scientific explanations within the physical realm are complete. Taking the second makes it a mistake to claim that complete explanations in the physical realm are purely scientific.

Thus science cannot generate *complete* explanations in terms of its characteristic concepts for the simple reason that it can give no account in those terms of the physical conditions it must assume in giving such explanations. But if such scientifically unexplained physical matters are to have some other sort of explanations, there seems to be no good reason to think that one might not need, for example, theological explanations to pick up those otherwise unexplained matters within the scientific level. If that should be the case, then the separation between religion and the scientific level has broken down and the original purpose of strict complementarity fails.

Even if all of that could be straightened out, the complementarity idea still faces difficulties. To achieve separation of science and religion the complementarist must maintain the independence of the various levels. However, the simple fact that complementary descriptions and explanations have reference to the same things seems to place some constraints on the independence of those explanations and descriptions. For instance, although scientific descriptions of the universe and claims about the purpose of the universe are on different levels (on this view), given the intricacy, expanse, variety and so on of the universe, we would probably not be too presumptuous in dismissing out of hand suggestions that the purpose of the universe is to produce used Volkswagen tires (which, of course, it in fact does). Surely there are constraints that one level levies on others. (In this context, think also of historical natural theology attempts to learn about God through scientific investigation of this world and of current arguments from some scientists that this universe is so precisely adjusted as to permit life that it cannot be a matter of chance. Here again, we seem to have cross-level connections and constraints.)

If the different levels of description concern the same things, laws on one level will apparently have parallels on other levels. Consider the case of human freedom and determinism, frequently cited by complementarists as a good example. Scientific determinism means, roughly, that there are certain sorts of events—call them A and B— such that when one occurs (A), the occurrence of the other (B) becomes inevitable. If human actions are determined scientifically, then the occurrence of certain scientifically describable events (electrochemical events in the brain, for instance) makes inevitable the occurrence of certain scientifically describable human actions.

But if those *events* themselves are so related, that sequence of *events* will occur, regardless of how they are *described*. Thus even if those events are described in some other level than the scientific, the sequence of *events* (now described in some different way—as thoughts, choices or whatever) will have the same inevitability as previously. The way we choose to describe things has no normative force for reality, and our choosing descriptions on different levels has no necessary bearing on the actual progress of the objective world, although it perhaps has great bearing on whether we see various connections on various levels. But if that is correct, then the complementarist claim that there is such independence between levels that it can be both true that we humans are subject to determinism on the scientific level but free on some other level[5] is simply mistaken.

We might expect that in similar fashion other patterns and features within the objects, processes and events describable in alternative and complementary ways would also show up characteristically described on the respective complementary levels.[6] If so, the independence between levels that this complementary picture requires to achieve the separation between science and religion for which it is intended, is lost.

It looks then as though neither the distinct-realm attempt nor the strict complementarity attempt will guarantee the separation of religion from science some Christians have sought. Perhaps it might be achieved in other ways, but suspicion of such separation has been increasing in the past two decades or so. Part of that suspicion has come from the influence of Kuhnian and Weltanschauung views, and some has arisen independently. If the separation is less than complete, then it may be possible and even legitimate for one's religious beliefs to affect one's science. That might occur in a number of ways and degrees.

Science and Religious Beliefs as Inseparably Blended

Some Christians have argued that each of one's beliefs affect the very content of each of the rest of one's beliefs. Some of them have further concluded that a believer and an unbeliever cannot even mean the same thing by such simple statements as $2 + 2 = 4$, since the believer will hold that belief as part of a total system that contains belief in God and commitment to him, while the unbeliever will hold the corresponding belief as part of a total system which does not contain that belief in God or that commitment.[7] On this view one's Christian beliefs will affect all the contents of one's science, since every scientific belief one has—either observational or theoretical—will be partially constituted by those religious beliefs. Christianity will then permeate the believer's science. And since the unbeliever's unbelief will permeate all of his science, there will be no points of contact between their sciences.

This view has several points in common with Kuhnian and Weltanschauung views, and it shares some of their problems as well. In particular, this type of view seems to lead to a powerful incommensurability between the sciences of believers and unbelievers. It appears to rule out communication and agreement between believing and unbelieving scientists. But such a division is not evident in practice. Believers and unbelievers work together scientifically, teach each other, learn from each other, use each other's results, talk to each other and write in the same journals. All of that seems difficult to reconcile with the position that they cannot share scientific beliefs or even talk the same language, since they cannot share meanings.

Of course, the unbeliever might accept some scientific theory as part of an overall posture of rebellion, and the acceptance of that theory might play some sort of role in that rebellion. A Christian might accept that same theory as part of an overall outlook of obedience and commitment, and acceptance of that theory might play some sort of role in that obedience and commitment. But those profoundly divergent contexts do not imply that the theory embedded in both is not one and the same, that the respective persons cannot agree on it, work together in a lab applying it and so forth, any more than one person's using an hour for prayer and another's using it for bank robbery means that they are on different time.

Science and Religious Belief as Related in Some Degree
Other Christians have rejected both of the above views and the epistemologies underlying them. In doing so, many of them have abandoned parts of the traditional view of science without having moved to the opposite end of the scale, thus leaving open the possibility of Christian belief affecting the content of science.

Theory choice. Some Christians have argued that various broad Christian principles are relevant to theory choice. As one example, some argue that the Christian belief in the sovereignty of God rules out theories that postulate irreducibly chance mechanisms in nature (perhaps of the sort that contemporary interpretations of quantum mechanics tend toward). On such positions it is not that Christians and non-Christians cannot mean or observe the same things, but that even on identical empirical bases Christian principles rule out some scientific interpretations of those commonly held empirical matters.[8]

Some who hold this position argue that Christian principles only come to bear in the human sciences, where moral responsibility or the doctrine of humans as created in God's image becomes relevant. Others argue that Christian beliefs affect various disciplines in different degrees—no effect in logic and mathematics, little in physics and chemistry, more in biology, more yet in psychology and sociology, and so forth.[9] Here again some components of the traditional view may be retained, but the wall of separation between Christian belief and science is breached at some point.

Limited complementarity. Another possible approach is to accept the basic complementarist idea that at least some of the same phenomena can be approached from both a scientific and a religious perspective, but to reject the strict complementarist idea that each perspective is in any important sense complete, since it was that claim of completeness that generated problems for the strict complementarity position.[10]

On this position one might admit that the ultimate *physical* initial conditions necessary in scientific explanations have to be explained in terms of some other category, for instance, the theological. One might further hold that the relevant *philosophical* principles essential to science (uniformity, simplicity, comprehendability, lawfulness) are also to be accounted for by appeal to the theological realm. One could then argue that *beyond* those starting points the two perspectives do not intermingle but deal with different concerns, different concepts and different types of explanations—just as the strict complementarist claims. Thus Christian belief as such would not dictate any of the content of scientific theory or stipulate any scientific facts but could be called on in explanations of the actual contours of some empirical facts about nature (the ultimate initial conditions) and in more basic explanations, for instance concerning why there are even any facts at all. This would again involve giving up claims of the completeness of scientific explanations (contrary to strict complementarism), but it would maintain the separation of the scientific and religious at all points beyond the primordial initial conditions.

Of course, maintaining that separation beyond the initial starting point amounts to claiming that the world is governed in such a way that once things are set going, religious themes never intrude into the normal workings of the world's internal mechanics in a manner inexplicable in the terms of natural scientific explanations. Those who are uncomfortable with that rather large assertion (and how might one go about supporting it?) might wish to adopt an even more restricted sort of complementarity, according to which many, *but not all,* phenomena coming after the start of creation are capable of complementary descriptions and explanations. For instance, some views of miracles might dictate this type of position. As another example, some people believe that human consciousness and self-consciousness are not explicable in naturalistic terms. If those people are correct, then some current phenomena with which we are acquainted cannot be given explanations from the perspective of the purely natural sciences. If that is the case, then not only can scientific explanations not be complete in the material realm, but they cannot even be complete in the natural realm restricted so as to exclude ultimate initial conditions.

Although this more limited complementarity is attractive, there are difficulties. A major attraction of complementarity is that it allows for peaceful nonaggression between naturalistic science and religious belief. But the areas into which complementarity would *not* extend if limited in the above way (ultimate beginnings, miracles, human self-consciousness) are exactly the areas most subject to controversy, exactly those areas in which the peace it wants to promise is needed most. Strict complementarity ensures the peace; but when its problematic completeness claims are given up, the trouble spots that made the complementarity truce attractive are the first to emerge. But that may just indicate that reality is not neatly compartmentalized.

In any case, the above *sorts* of views fit comfortably with many contemporary conceptions of science. Those conceptions recognize that considerations other than the bare empirical are relevant to science and that there is a hard core of reality that refuses to roll over and play dead before our prior scientific and nonscientific prejudices and which thus must intrude into everyone's science, thereby putting some firm constraints on the effects of some of these other influences. Exactly what all the common constraints are is still a matter for discussion, but arbitrary attempts to argue that science *cannot* properly be influenced at any juncture by one's Christian commitment and beliefs will have to be defended on their own terms, not on the basis of out-dated conceptions of science.

Science and Scripture

Scripture is another *possible* source of input into science for the Christian. Here again, there is a wide range of views taken by Christians—from there being no input whatever to there being controlling input. We will consider a number of positions growing out of two different views on the proper interpretation and use of Scripture.

Scripture as having no internal scientific relevance. Even if one accepted the traditional picture of science, there could be a distinc-tively Christian science if Scripture contained empirical data, or scien-tific principles, or specific constraints on theories, which Christians incorporated into their science and others did not. To maintain a sepa-ration of science and Scripture (and of science and religion), one must either deny that Scripture contains any such information or deny that it is legitimate to use it in science even if any is there. Let us take those alternatives in reverse order.

A number of people (including some Christians) think that whether or not there is scientifically relevant information in Scripture, one should not appeal to Scripture in the scientific context. There seems to be two distinct reasons behind the view, one philosophical and the other pragmatic.

The first of those reasons is the view that science must *by definition* be naturalistic and that everything that goes into science must come from purely natural methods.[11] Thus even if Scripture does contain empirical data or constraints on theorizing and the like, we are not to use it qua scientists.

That is an initially surprising position. If the object of science is to learn truth about the world, then surely it would be counterproductive to place restrictions on where such truths can come from, so long as we are *rationally* justified in accepting them. If Scripture does indeed give us relevant empirical facts or the outline of a proper scientific theory, what is the point in adopting a policy of pretending as a scien-tist that we do not have the information? If science were a rule-bound game, with the object of seeing how much we could learn while operating under a variety of imposed limitations, then it might be interesting to see how far one could get if restricted to information that could be acquired naturalistically. But if science is more than just this sort of game, there must be some sort of *epistemic justification* for any restrictions of this sort placed on it.

The natural place to look for such justification would be in a theory of confirmation, showing that the best available methods for pursuing truth in science dictated those limitations. But appeal to theories of confirmation will not at the moment settle the issue. For one thing, there is still live dispute in the area of confirmation theory, and not all of the currently proposed alternatives rule out appeal to Scripture. Even some of those that might rule out appeal to Scripture leave open the possibility of future reversals of such restrictions. For another, as discussed earlier, contemporary thought concerning confirmations tends to construe confirmation as involving application of epistemic values, and the resulting decisions will often not be rigidly dictated decisions. It may thus be quite difficult to show decisively that appeal to Scripture in science is either improper or irrational, or that adopting conformity to Scripture as an epistemic value is either improper or irrational.

But many Christians would argue that there is good pragmatic justification for not appealing to Scripture for scientific data and constraints on theorizing.[12] On their view the history of science is not only the history of discovery concerning nature but also of discovery concerning which epistemic values are most effective. Although epistemic values are not results of science, there is still philosophical feedback from the shape of scientific results achieved by the use of specific epistemic values to those underlying values themselves. Thus epistemic values can be modified and rearranged in ways having indirect relation to scientific results. (Nevertheless the modifications and rearrangements that take place are also value influenced.) If we look at the history of science, the argument continues, we see that for the most part whenever scientists have attempted to incorporate what was taken to be scientific information from Scripture into their science, they ended up with unfruitful theories and positions. Thus in the *natu-*

ral sciences conformity to Scripture has not fared well as an epistemic value, although in the human sciences it may be a different matter.

But the real problem is *not* that adherence to what Scripture teaches has been scientifically unproductive. Given that what Scripture teaches is *true,* incorporating what Scripture teaches into science could hardly be counterproductive. The real problem is that incorporating what people have *thought* Scripture teaches into science has (at least according to many) been counterproductive. And I think that what has prompted many Christians to want to bar appeal to Scripture from science has been the belief that even if Scripture does contain scientifically relevant data, *we* may not know what is being taught as scientific data and what is not. In fact, some argue that such a judgment is one we can make only *after* we have done our scientific work.[13] For instance, it was only *after* the revolution in astronomy in the sixteenth and seventeenth centuries that the church saw that scriptural phrases concerning the motionlessness of the earth were not to be taken as providing scientific data.

If in general we only know what in Scripture is scientific data and what is not after we have done the relevant scientific work, then adopting conformity with our *antecedent* reading of Scripture as an epistemic value may have unpromising results. And if that is correct, the argument continues, perhaps we are better off taking the long (scientific) way around than trying to take (scriptural) short-cuts that may through our incorrect interpretations take us off the proper track.

But that is not to say that there is anything either scientifically improper or irrational per se in holding a set of epistemic values that contains *conformity to Scripture,* and in trying to construct one's science on that basis. That, in fact, is what some contemporary creationists have attempted to do.[14] They have taken conformity to a fairly literal reading of Scripture as one of their most important epistemic values. Critics frequently claim that creationists have not managed to make much theoretical progress from that context and have not met various criteria (fruitfulness, breadth of scope, etc.) Some Christians argue that those are not serious criticisms, either because in our finitude we cannot expect to get far in understanding the creation, or perhaps because there just has not been time to get all such matters worked out yet on a contemporary creationist basis. In any case, such Christians argue, adherence to Scripture interpreted fairly literally is what is demanded of us as Christians whether in science or out of science, so that is where we must begin.

There is nothing fundamentally irrational or even unscientific in principle in such a position, although such positions can be defended or perhaps developed in ways neither rational nor scientific. But creationists cannot justifiably claim that their approach is the only *scientific* approach, that they are the only ones really following the "rules" of science, that mainstream science is basically confused or that their science really does what mainstream science only says it is trying to do. What we have here are separate, partially overlapping but different projects, and their differences are consequences of much deeper value differences.

Although few Christians deny that Scripture contains contextually relevant information—that the world is a creation, for instance—several groups maintain that Scripture contains no specific, scientifically relevant information. Liberals and modernists have taken Scripture to be purely human records, either records of the events in which God reveals himself or records of human attempts to find God. In either case, Scripture would not be authoritative; and if it contained anything even purportedly scientifically relevant, there would be no particular scientific reason to pay it any attention, and thus it would not need to affect one's science.

There are at least two other ways of maintaining that Scripture has no scientific implications. Some have held that Scripture makes no scientific claims of any sort, that the passages that *look* as though they are scientifically relevant (statements about the flood or about the length of time of creation) are purely poetic (or some other sort of non-indicative language) and in reality assert only spiritual truths—for instance, who created and why, and not how he created or what (in any detail) he created, that question being left to science.[15] If such a view is correct, then any appearance of scientifically relevant matters in Scripture is only appearance, and if Scripture is read properly, one will find nothing bearing on the content of science.

Another way is to interpret Scripture as containing statements that would, if true, have scientific relevance but to construe such statements as things that the human writers of Scripture might have believed but which God did not intend to teach us and which therefore we do not have to take as binding on our belief.[16] On this view the message God gives in Scripture may be wrapped in ways that include beliefs of the culture and context in which the message was given, but we are required to conform our thinking only to the core of the message, not its cultural wrappings. On this view also if we read Scripture correctly, we will find nothing to which our specific theories must conform.

A key point here is that these cases for separation must rest on how we interpret Scripture. It will not do to appeal to traditional views of science as support for such a separation for two reasons. First, even if traditional views were correct, this type of separation would not follow automatically. Second, as we saw earlier, the traditional views of science are not correct in any case.

Scripture as containing extractable scientifically relevant information. Naturally enough, those who hold that Scripture has determinable implication for the content of science often hold quite different views of Scripture from those just depicted. First are those who advocate taking as strict a literal reading on all matters as one can.[17] On that approach there will be much in Scripture to which the Christian should conform his or her science that will be inconsistent with much of contemporary mainstream science. (Consider, here, the age of the earth, the length of time between the appearance of lower life forms and the appearance of humans, the origin of the human race, the extent of the flood and so on.) With even a fairly traditional conception of science, this view of Scripture will yield effects on the content of science. In fact, many creationists have a quite positivistic conception of science and simply put the results of their reading of Scripture into that context.[18]

Others believe that Scripture contains scientific truths in a literal but nonspecific form, although getting at it takes more than just a straightforward reading. For instance, some terms in Scripture may be ambiguous (versus poetic or metaphorical), and once those ambiguities are straightened out, what Scripture is then seen to say even on scientific matters is to be taken as literally true.[19] For example, it is sometimes argued that the term translated "day" in Genesis 1 can refer to indeterminately long stretches of time and that if we take this as being the literal meaning of the term in the context, then what Genesis tells us is literally true, that is, there were six indeterminately long creative periods (the day-age view, for instance).[20] On this interpretation also, Scripture can play a substantive role within a Christian's science.

There is another possible style of scriptural interpretation. In this view Scripture does indeed contain scientifically relevant information but only indirectly or metaphorically. For instance it might be held that none of the specific details of the Genesis account of origins is to be taken literally in any sense, but the presence of all of that apparent detail tells us that chance-based accounts of origins are unacceptable, and therefore any such scientific theory is mistaken.[21] Thus there is a scientific message there, on this view, but it is not the message that one might think on the basis of a straight literal reading or of word studies.

If any of the above ways of construing Scripture is correct, then Scripture will indeed contain material with consequences for the content of science. We would then expect the science of Christians to be different from that of those who did not accept the authority of Scripture, unless they could independently discover the same scientific material contained in Scripture, as some Christians believe possible.

Moral Constraints

One additional relationship between Christianity and science is that there are moral constraints on the Christian in science that might not be observed by non-Christians. For instance, many Christians believe that human life begins at conception or fertilization and that the taking of human life is wrong. But if life begins that early, then research on in vitro fertilization, for instance, which routinely involves the destruction of fertilized human ova, thus becomes a moral and not merely a scientific issue for Christians. Most of us can construct lists of other areas of possible scientific research from which a Christian would be morally barred. (As a start, consider research concerning human physiological reactions to undergoing involuntary torture in the lab.) Some

Christians also believe that even "pure" research is out of bounds for the Christian in cases where the most reasonable expectation is that the results of such research will be employed for either immoral or destructive purposes.

We thus cannot claim that all that science gives rise to—that all the ways in which scientific method can be applied in principle, that the discovering of every discoverable truth and that all the things that a scientist might do—are morally neutral and permissible just in virtue of being "scientific." Whatever one concludes about the relationship of Christian belief and Scripture to the *contents* of science, we cannot escape the relevance of God's commands to the *conduct* of science.

Concerning Science, Belief and Scripture

Disputes concerning whether and to what degree Christianity ought to affect science, or whether Christian science is or ought to be different from non-Christian science, must be settled in part on the basis of answers to questions concerning the proper reading of Scripture. As indicated earlier one cannot simply say that there should be no difference and appeal for support merely to a traditional view of science. On the other side of the issue, we cannot argue that Christian belief and acceptance of Scripture inevitably affect one's science and try to base that position solely on Kuhnian or Weltanschauung conceptions of science. What of more contemporary pictures of science?

As noted, such views at least leave open the possibility of interaction between Christianity and the internal working of science. Many contemporary views stress the importance of background beliefs and values as the context out of which theorizing and interpretation of data grow. Although there is dispute over what is or is not a proper background constituent, prohibitions on Christians taking what God has said as part of the landscape on which their science is erected surely require justification. And if God has indeed revealed to us truths concerning the world he created, surely Christians do not want to deny those truths in their science, and given that Christians want their science to ultimately conform to what God has said, systematically ignoring what he has said also requires justification, to say the least.

Even if there are distinctive features of Christian science, there could be overlap or even near identity of content between Christian and non-Christian science. There will, however, be substantial differences in the significance assigned to science seen as investigating God's creation versus investigating "just one of those things that sometimes happen." To paraphrase George Marsden, nonbelievers may hear all the notes of science, but without the theistic context and perspective they will not hear the song.

Appendix

Speaking the Truth in Love
Some Thoughts About Feet

Almost from its beginning the Christian community has had internal differences over both doctrines and practices. We have been warned that it is partly through our treatment of fellow believers that we as Christians are to be known, but despite that fact our treatment of those with whom we have disagreements has not always been exactly sterling. How then *should* we conduct ourselves toward other Christians with whom we have serious disagreements—disagreements over issues that we take to have real religious significance? What principles should govern that conduct?

We should take our cue, I think, from Ephesians 4:14-16:

> Then we will no longer be infants, tossed back and forth by the waves, and blown here and there by every wind of teaching and by the cunning and craftiness of men in their deceitful scheming. Instead, speaking the truth in love, we will in all things grow up into him who is the Head, that is, Christ. From him the whole body, joined and held together by every supporting ligament, grows and builds itself up in love, as each part does its work.

We are to *speak* the *truth* in *love*. Each of those three terms has something to tell us. Let us look at each in turn.

Speak

Speaking is one sign and one function of community. Indeed, one way we indicate that community has been fractured is by saying that we are "not speaking to her anymore" or that we are "not on speaking terms with him." But together we are supposed to constitute one community, one body, and as part of that body we are to maintain that communion; we are speak to each other—the truth in love. If we break that communion, if we sever some part of that body, if we refuse to speak either by shunning or by shouting (or by silencing other voices), we not only lose that part, we may impair the functioning of the whole body.

The old comic strip *Pogo* was about a group of animals living in a swamp in Georgia. In one episode a group of them were discussing a lucky charm—a rabbit's foot. One of the group, a rabbit, was deeply moved and spoke feelingly about the poor rabbit who had given a foot so that someone could have good luck. Another member of the group, a fox, insisted that the rabbit had it all wrong—that one should not feel sorry for or be impressed by the rabbit for giving the foot but should feel sympathy for and be impressed by the foot, which after all had given its whole rabbit.

That is a danger when one begins to play with breaking community, when one toys with amputation—one *might* end up on the wrong side of the cut. Historically there have been Christian groups very much like that foot. In setting themselves strictly apart from others who did not see things exactly as they did, they have in effect cut themselves off from the body of believers. For instance, earlier in this century a number of creationists thought that they could more effectively promote their views if they formed an organization and pooled resources and coordinated their efforts. All were conservative, believing, committed Christians. But the organization plan hit a serious snag when it was suggested that they begin their first meeting with prayer. The members from one group had some differences with another group represented there and refused to engage in joint prayer with them. That first group, it seems to me, was being a foot industriously engaged in sawing off the rest of the rabbit.

Of course, there may be situations where amputation is necessary to save the rest of the body—when one *has* to break communion. But those occasions may be rarer than many suppose. Paul notes (Rom 14:5-13) that some Christians honor one day, some another, some none—and indicates that this type of difference is not enough to break communion with other Christians. Although that might sound to some like a trivial issue, think of the context. Sabbath observance was deeply woven into Jewish beliefs, Jewish traditions and Jewish life. As doctrine, Sabbath observance was theologically linked to the creation. As practice and tradition, it had been meticulously followed for centuries. As a command, its violation in the Old Testament was punished by death. Sabbath observance was not a casual, inconsequential, tangential matter. Yet Paul says that disagreement in both practice and doctrine on that point was not sufficient to justify breaking communion, at least in the sense of refusing to recognize as a fellow Christian anyone with whom one disagreed on this issue. This previously capital matter was not important enough to sever part of the body.

Again, breaking communion may sometimes have to be done, but we should be hesitant and should at least *think* about whether we are being the foot that saws off its rabbit. Because although the rabbit may end up limping, the foot will not make it at all.

Truth

In our disagreements we are to speak the *truth*—not casual opinions, not what everyone knows, not half-baked plausibilities. We are obviously not infallible in our quests for truth, but we must at least *try* to get at truth as best we can, and that means that we are obligated to do our homework before we say very much. Let me briefly mention a couple illustrations from the creation/evolution dispute. There are many sides to that dispute even within the Christian community, but young-earth creationism and theistic evolution are probably the most visible. Let us look at each in turn in connection with the general idea of doing homework.

Theistic evolution: some homework. Five years after publication of

Darwin's *Origin of Species,* eight scientists (several of whom were destined to be among the most influential of the period) formed the X Club, with the aims of promoting the growth and social authority of science and in particular of freeing science from any domination by religion. The members of the club generally embraced philosophical naturalism, and for some the fight against religion went much farther then merely evicting it from the domain of science. In that broader conflict some within the X Club saw the *Origin* as a major piece of antireligious artillery—Thomas Huxley, for instance, referred to it as "a veritable Whitworth gun in the armoury of liberalism."[1] And Karl Marx (not linked to the club) was so pleased with Darwinism and the potential he thought it exhibited for the cause of antisupernaturalism that he wanted to dedicate the English translation of *Das Kapital* to Darwin.

Such episodes represent a fairly strong historical thread of attempts to co-opt evolution as a worldview weapon against religious belief. In fact, such attempts continue to the present. The National Association of Biology Teachers recently issued the following statement:

> The diversity of life on earth is the outcome of evolution: an unsupervised, impersonal, unpredictable and natural process of temporal descent with genetic modification that is affected by natural selection, chance, historical contingencies and changing environments.

Although very quickly modified, that original statement—"unsupervised, impersonal"—implies that *by definition* evolution means that no one is in charge here.[2]

Such purported implications may not be a *formal* part of evolutionary biological theory (I do not believe that they are), nor may they *strictly* follow from the biological theory proper (I do not believe that they do). But there has been a historically, widely felt smooth interlocking—clicking into place—between Darwinian evolution and opposition to religion, and that is not necessarily just "sheer Fundamentalist fantasy" either.[3] That perceived fit is what Oxford Professor Richard Dawkins referred to in his famous remark that

> Darwin made it possible to be an intellectually fulfilled atheist.[4]

And as Thomas Nagel put it,

> Darwin enabled modern secular culture to heave a great collective sigh of relief, by apparently providing a way to eliminate purpose, meaning, and design as fundamental features of the world.[5]

The operative supposition underlying the above episodes and quotes is that science can sometimes have genuine worldview implications and that the implications in this case (evolution) are not happy ones for religious belief. But opponents of religious belief are not the only ones to have suspected some deep tensions here—many lay Christians and many creationists have as well.

Some theistic evolutionists, however, have rejected that worry of other Christians, arguing that evolution *cannot* have any deep worldview implications because science is strictly empirical and when things are properly compartmentalized, nonempirical matters such as religion and worldviews are completely walled off from, completely disconnected from, completely immune to, anything science could ever say. In this they echo, for example, Tillich, who remarks that

> Scientific truth and the truth of faith do not belong to the same dimension of meaning. Science has no right and no power to interfere with faith and faith has no power to interfere with science.[6]

But as we saw earlier, the positivist view of science that typically flavors such positions has been *known* to be inadequate for nearly half a century. According to more contemporary understandings of science the possibility of deep connections between scientific theories, scientifically essential presuppositions and broader matters cannot be simply dismissed wholesale. In specific cases there may well be no conflict, but that cannot be established merely by wielding sweeping categorizations—science over here, religion over there.

Those Christians (and those opponents of religion) who believe that evolution and Christian belief are in conflict may be mistaken. And those theistic evolutionists who believe that there is no conflict may be right. But anyone who grounds that "no conflict" position in an exploded conception of what science is, needs to find a firmer footing. And that means doing some philosophy of science homework[7]—and perhaps some worldview warfare homework as well.

Creationism: Some Homework.

Much of the conservative Christian community has been seriously misled concerning what Darwinian evolutionary theory actually says, what the relevant scientific evidence is, what that evidence does or does not show about evolution, and concerning what science is and how it works. Following are two brief examples, one involving philosophy of science, the other involving the content of Darwinian theory.

1. Philosophy of science. Quite a number of popular creationists take their philosophy of science explicitly from the *Oxford Dictionary:*

> A branch of study which is concerned either with a connected body of demonstrated truths or with observed facts systematically classified and more or less colligated by being brought under general laws, and which includes trustworthy methods for the discovery of new truth within its own domain.[8]

As should be clear by now, that definition misses few opportunities to embrace long-refuted positions. Science, of course, does not *"demonstrate"* truths in any strict sense of the term. Worse yet, if one began with "observed facts," then "systematically classified" them (evidently by some Baconian means) by "bringing them under general laws," one would never get beyond empirical generalizations to *theoretical* understanding of those data at all. Recall that there simply is no *logic of discovery.* There are no automatic "trustworthy methods" for discovering new truths—especially for getting from the empirical level to the theoretical. If there were, the creativity of scientists would not be nearly as crucial to science as it is. This conception of science has essentially all the difficulties of the Baconianism that it evidently reflects.

Beyond that, popular creationist pictures of science frequently include mistakes concerning the natures of and relationships between theories and data, the nature of and scope of *testability* and *falsifiability,* the status and effects of anomalous observations, the implications of the existence of alternative theoretical interpretations, the nature and role of the concepts of *observability* and *reproducibility* and so on.[9]

2. Darwinian content. Creationist popularizers frequently have an inadequate grasp of current evolutionary theory. For instance, a number confuse Darwinian evolution with earlier theories of evolution (especially that of Lamarck, who died thirty years before Darwin's publication of the *Origin of Species*). Failure to distinguish Darwin from Lamarck is quite common among creationist popularizers, despite the facts that the differences are not just in superficial detail but are fundamental and that Darwin himself explicitly rejected the structure, basis, underlying principles and mechanism of Lamarckian evolution (referring to some parts of it as "nonsense"). Many popular creationist criticisms might well point to real difficulties in Lamarck's theories. But the problem is that Lamarck's theories have been rejected by the scientific community for two-thirds of a century, and that given the deep differences between Darwinian and Lamarckian evolution, criticisms relevant to Lamarckian theories often have no bearing at all on Darwinian theories. The creationists in question have not done sufficient work even to discover that they are often attacking a theory that no one actually holds, that few have held it for generations and that the attacks miss the *real* theory entirely.[10]

Unfortunately, such confusions have had consequences. Creationist popularizers are often accepted as authorities by thousands of Christians—sometimes by influential hosts of religious television programs. Thus, many well-meaning lay Christians and ministers have been substantially misled as to what evolutionary (and other) theories actually say and misled as to the alleged trivial ease with which evolution can be refuted. Beyond that, such fundamental mistakes by some visible creationists have tarred the whole movement and have thus made it more difficult for other creationists who are attempting to construct legitimate science from a creationist perspective to get serious consideration.

Upshot. For both sides, failure to do the homework generates real risks—first, the risk of speaking something other than the truth, and second, the risk of getting caught flat-footed in a variety of embarrassing errors. And the louder you have trumpeted those errors and the larger they turn out to be and the more obvious it becomes that you have not done your homework, the more embarrassing it can be. And rest assured that if one is speaking to a competent practitioner from the opposite side, those errors will be instantly spotted and the fact that you have your foot stuffed firmly in your mouth will be duly pointed out to you—and to everyone else as well. And that is not where our feet are supposed to be. We are supposed to know the truth and to firmly *stand,* with both feet on the ground stablizing us against the winds that try to blow us around.

Love

Sometimes even when both sides have done their homework, disagreement persists. What then? Having done your homework, being *responsibly* convinced that you are right, the temptation is to take aim at your disagreeing brother or sister and blow 'em away—with the truth, of course.

But if we have not sawed off our entire rabbit, then we are still one body—you may be hands, someone else eyes, your opponent may be a foot. They—the foot—are part of the same body you are part of. And that means that blazing away at one's fellow believer may be, in effect, shooting one's self in one's own foot. We are to love others as ourselves, and since we are *one body,* our usual reluctance to open fire on our own foot thus has consequences for our proposed firing at fellow believers. Since we are reluctant to shoot *ourselves* in the foot, we should not shoot them—either *in* the foot or *as* a foot.

Does that mean that we should not pursue disagreements? That we should not try to convince others of their errors? No—we are, after all, to *speak* the truth.

But it must be in love. Suppose that in something like the creation-evolution case you really *do* have the truth—your side really is right. If you speak it, but *not* in love, what does Scripture say about you? It does not congratulate you for speaking that truth—even Balaam's donkey spoke truth. It does not give you permission to vilify those with whom you disagree. It does not applaud you for your insistence on correcting those around you. The Pharisees do not get a lot of extra credit in Scripture. In 1 Corinthians 13:2 Paul says:

> If I have the gift of prophecy and can fathom all mysteries and all knowledge, and if I have a faith that can move mountains, but have not love, I am nothing.

So if you know not only the truth about origins and creation and evolution but even about all mysteries, but lack love, you are nothing.

How *does* love do it? We are given a description and a model. The description is in 1 Corinthians 13:4-7:

> Love is patient, love is kind. It does not envy, it does not boast, it is not proud. It is not rude, it is not self-seeking, it is not easily angered, it keeps no record of wrongs. Love does not delight in evil but rejoices with the truth. It always protects, always trusts, always hopes, always perseveres.

The model? In John 13:34, Christ says:

> A new command I give you: Love one another. As I have loved you, so you must love one another.

That is not always easy. For instance, after having gotten nailed on something we vociferously held but that turned out to be wrong, how many of us rejoice that the truth of our opponent has now triumphed over our own error? And how often do we speak truth in superiority? in scorn? or as a weapon? And how often do we make other views and motives easier to attack by not reading them charitably? And how often do we really love those aggravatingly confused and obnoxiously bullheaded people on the other side of our issues who simply refuse to see it the right way—our way? But that is what we are supposed to do—love.

Of course, sometimes there may really be something about some other part of the body that does require serious corrective action. But we must be careful how we go about it. A few years ago a woman who had been troubled by a very painful corn on her foot decided to fix it permanently. Being completely plastered with wine at the time, her choice of surgical instrument was a bit questionable—a shotgun. The treatment was effective—the corn was indeed removed, and she has not been subsequently bothered by it.

But nonetheless, as can be imagined the story did not have a completely happy ending. After all, she literally shot herself in the foot. And if we Christians are one body, then in correcting our fellow believer with a shotgun we may be shooting ourselves in the foot after all. And the ending may be just as unsatisfactory.

Disagreements

One final issue. Disagreements are not necessarily a sign of something gone wrong. They need not be feared. Sometimes they can even be positive signs—signs of life. There are some things in Scripture that sometimes seem to point simultaneously in different directions, and we may not know quite how to put everything together. With many of the major historical disputes of the church—like predestination versus free choice, for instance—*both* sides were firmly rooted in Scripture, and the dispute arose because the two groups had taken hold of different pieces of the larger picture or different poles of what looked like a tension. But in such cases, the fact that there *is* a dispute means that both sides have gotten hold of something in Scripture—which is good—and are defending it as faithfully and committedly as they can—which is good—and are not going to be easily dislodged from that truth—which is also good.

And sometimes disputes are an opportunity to learn, to grow. They can be part of the very process by which some of our crucial homework gets done—by which we learn some of the truth.

Sometimes *both* sides end up being better for having had the disagreement. Proverbs 27:17 says: "Iron sharpens iron, so one man sharpens another."

So raise the tough issues with your opponent. Ask the tough questions. Probe their position. Speak the truth. But do it to *sharpen* them, to *strengthen* them—and not just because they disagree with you and thus obviously deserve to be clobbered. Recall the passage at the beginning, Ephesians 4:

> Instead, speaking the truth in love, we will in all things grow up into him who is the Head, that is, Christ. From him the whole body, joined and held together by every supporting ligament, grows and builds itself up in love, as each part does its work.

That is the object—we are to grow, and the body is to grow and to be built up in love. And it is in *your* interest for those you disagree with to be stronger—after all, they and you are *ultimately* of the same body, and in a body, in a genuine community, the weakness of one can affect all.

Ask the tough questions of *yourself* too. That is part of doing the homework. And *listen* to the questions and answers of your opponent. You just might discover that your own house has a shakier footing than you thought. And finding that out is in your—and the community's—interest as well.

Conclusion

So—three principles concerning disputes within the Christian community:

1. Speak	Do not break community lightly. Do not be the foot that cuts off its whole rabbit.
2. the truth	Do the homework. Do not get caught with your scientific or theological or philosophical foot in your mouth. That not only hampers speaking, it makes it difficult to use both feet to stand firm.
3. in love.	Do not, by shooting fellow members of the body, thereby shoot yourself in the foot. Do not trim corns with a shotgun.

So speak the truth in love. And it seems to me that in many of our frequent internal disputes, the greatest of these is love.

Notes

Chapter 2. The Traditional Conception of Science

[1]Bacon's views are developed in his *Novum Organum,* especially the second book, beginning with section 10.

[2]See, for example, Carl Hempel, *Philosophy of Natural Science* (Englewood Cliffs, N.J.: Prentice-Hall, 1966), pp. 11-18. Criticisms of Baconianism discussed here largely follow Hempel.

[3]Useful survey and discussion of the sorts of views that were dominant in earlier parts of this century (prior to the sixties) are contained in Frederick Suppe, *The Structure of Scientific Theories* (Urbana: University of Illinois Press, 1977), and Harold I. Brown, *Perception, Theory and Commitment* (Chicago: University of Chicago Press, 1977).

[4]See, for example, Hilary Putnam, *Reason, Truth and History* (Cambridge: Cambridge University Press, 1981), pp. 124-25.

[5]Hempel, *Philosophy of Natural Science,* chap. 5. Also Ernest Nagel, *The Structure of Science* (New York: Harcourt, Brace & World, 1961), chap. 3; and Carl Hempel's *Aspects of Scientific Explanation* (New York: Free Press, 1965), chap. 10.

[6]Hempel, *Philosophy of Natural Science,* pp. 6-9; *Aspects,* chap. 1.

[7]Hempel, *Philosophy of Natural Science,* p. 31, for example.

[8]Ibid., p. 16, for example.

[9]Some of its better-known members were Moritz Schlick, Rudolph Carnap, Otto Neurath and Herbert Feigl. Also associated with it were such people as Hans Reichenbach and Carl Hempel. Essays by most of these plus several others can be found in A. J. Ayer, ed., *Logical Positivism* (New York: Free Press, 1959).

[10]A sort of "official" statement of positivist style views is A. J. Ayer, *Language, Truth and Logic* (New York: Dover, 1946).

[11]Ibid., pp. 35-40.

[12]Brown, *Perception, Theory and Commitment,* pt. 1, contains good discussion of the positivist attempts to subsume various parts of science under symbolic logic and the ensuing difficulties. See also Suppe, *Structure of Scientific Theories,* pp. 6-15. See also Dudley Shapere, "Meaning and Scientific Change," *Scientific Revolutions,* ed. Ian Hacking (Oxford: Oxford University Press, 1981), pp. 28-32.

[13]The most extensive work on probability by a member of this group was probably that of Rudolph Carnap.

[14]See Ayer, *Language, Truth and Logic,* pp. 41-42 and chap. 6.

[15]Ayer adopts a phenomenalist position, that one can "define material things in terms of sense-contents." Ibid., p. 53.

[16]Ibid., p. 48.

[17]See again Suppe and Brown for discussions.

[18]Some philosophers argue that such a project *could not* succeed. See Putnam, *Reason, Truth and History,* p. 125.

[19]For a good summary discussion of technical difficulties with the Verifiability Criterion, see Alvin Plantinga, *God and Other Minds* (Ithaca, N.Y.: Cornell University Press, 1967), pp. 156-68.

[20]Popper's best known works are *The Logic of Scientific Discovery* (1934; reprinted, New York: Harper, 1959); and *Conjectures and Refutations* (New York: Harper, 1963, 1965). There is a large literature on Popper: for example, Brown, *Perception, Theory and Commitment,* chap. 5; and W. H. Newton-Smith, *The Rationality of Science* (Boston: Routledge and Kegan Paul, 1981) chap. 3.

[21]Popper, *Logic of Scientific Discovery,* p. 252.

[22]For example, ibid., p. 33.

[23]For example, ibid., pp. 63, 70.

[24]For example, ibid., pp. 29, 30, 33. See also Popper, *Conjectures and Refutations,* p. 40.

[25]For example, Popper, *Logic of Scientific Discovery,* pp. 29, 40.

[26]Ibid., p. 257. Popper repeats that passage in *Conjectures and Refutations,* p. 281 n. 67.

[27]Popper, *Logic of Scientific Discovery,* p. 364. See also pp. 278, 330.

[28]If universal statements have a probability of zero, then the existential statements that constitute their negations will have a probability of 1. That result has seemed wildly counterintuitive to many (see, e.g., Alvin Plantinga, *Warrant and Proper Function* [New York: Oxford, 1993], pp. 148-49). However, Popper accepts it. See for example, Popper, *Conjectures and Refutations* pp. 249 and 277 n. 57a.

[29]Popper, *Logic of Scientific Discovery,* p. 40.

[30]Popper, *Conjectures and Refutations,* p. 228.

[31]Popper, *Logic of Scientific Discovery,* p. 278.

[32]This inference involves the logically legitimate inference form known as *modus tollens.* The actual falsification situation is, however, not as simple as this claim makes it seem, as will be seen later.

[33]A particularly clear example of that comes from biologist Paul Gross and mathematician Norman Levitt, in their *Higher Superstition* (Baltimore: Johns Hopkins, 1998). On p. 86 we find the following:

> [T]he no-nonsense logical positivism adumbrated in such influential books as A. J. Ayer's *Language, Truth and Logic* was widely discussed and supported. It is safe to say that some version of this viewpoint—with Popperian addenda—is still embraced, at least tentatively by most working scientists who have reflected at all (as most have) on the issues of knowing and truth.

Not only does that apparently constitute an endorsement of logical positivism, it completely overlooks the fact that Popper rejected nearly every core doctrine of logical positivism.

[34]Popper, *Logic of Scientific Discovery,* pp. 108, 109. Popper believed that the special, falsifying data statements ("basic statements") were falsifiable but that actually pursuing the relevant tests led to a regress. We escaped that regress by choosing (by convention) some stopping point. See, for example, pp. 104-6.

[35]Ibid., pp. 37-38, 53.

[36]Ibid., p. 111.

[37]There are a number of more complicated types of cases for which falsification fails as well.

[38]See, for example, Popper, *Conjectures and Refutations,* p. 249, and especially p. 277 n. 57a. See also Popper, *Logic of Scientific Discovery,* p. 69: "Strictly existential statements . . . cannot be falsified. . . . [N]o statement of an observed event . . . can contradict the existential statement 'There are white ravens.' . . . I shall therefore have to treat strictly existential statements as non-empirical or 'metaphysical'."

[39]The reference here is to Kuhn, whose views are discussed in chapter 3. Although the new challenge comes in part from a different direction, there are extremely close connections between Kuhn's and Popper's views. See for instance Kuhn's and Popper's contributions to Imre Lakatos and Alan Musgrave, eds., *Criticism and the Growth of Knowledge* (Cambridge: Cambridge University Press, 1970).

Chapter 3. Philosophy of Science in the 1960s & 1970s

[1]David Hume, *An Enquiry Concerning Human Understanding,* sect. 4, pt. 2. Widely available in, for example, *The Empiricists* (Garden City, N.Y.: Dolphin, 1961), pp. 327-33.

[2]Immanuel Kant, *Critique of Pure Reason,* trans. Norman Kemp Smith (New York: St. Martin's Press, 1965). See especially the section entitled "Transcendental Analytic," bk. 2, ch. 2, section 3, second analogy (p. 218). Note particularly paragraphs A 194, B 239, p. 222. See also A 190-91, B 235-36, p. 219; A 80, B 106, p. 113; and sections 1 and 2 of the "Transcendental Aesthetic," pp. 67, 74. Secondary sources are often helpful in understanding Kant's work.

[3]John A. Wheeler, "The Universe as Home for Man," *American Scientist* 62 (November-December 1964): 683-91, esp. 688-90. For discussion of the anthropic principle see, for example, Ernan McMullin, "How Should Cosmology Relate to Theology?" *The Sciences and Theology in the Twentieth Century,* ed. A. R. Peacocke (Notre Dame: Notre Dame Press, 1981), chap. 2.

[4]Thomas Kuhn, *The Structure of Scientific Revolutions* (Chicago: University of Chicago Press, 1962).

[5]Ibid., postscript, pp. 182-87.

[6]Ibid., pp. 22, 108.

[7]Ibid., chap. 3 and p. 37, for example.

[8]Ibid., pp. 24-34.

[9]Ibid., p. 34.

[10]Ibid., p. 10.

[11]Ibid., see chap. 4.

[12]Ibid., p. 52.

[13]Ibid., p. 64.

[14]Ibid., p. 82.

[15]Ibid., see chaps. 7 and 8.

[16]Ibid., pp. 82-83.

[17]Ibid., p. 84.

[18]Ibid., p. 79.

[19]Ibid., see chaps. 6 and 10, and p. 150, for example.

[20]Ibid. For some examples, see pp. 56, 64-65.

[21]Ibid., chap. 10, especially the first fifteen pages.

[22]Ibid., pp. 102, 149. See also Kuhn, "Reflections on My Critics," in *Criticism and the Growth of Knowledge,* ed. Imre Lakatos and Alan Musgrove (Cambridge: Cambridge University Press, 1970), pp. 231-78, especially pp. 266-67.

[23]Kuhn, *Structures of Scientific Revolutions,* for example, pp. 109, 148, 150. See also Kuhn, "Objectivity, Value Judgement and Theory Choice," in *The Essential Tension* (Chicago: University of Chicago Press, 1977).

[24]Kuhn, *Structure of Scientific Revolutions,* pp. 103, 109.

[25]Ibid., pp. 94, 108.

[26]Ibid., pp. 106, 110-11, 117-18, 120-21, 134-35, 150, for example.

[27]Ibid., p. 121, for example. Kuhn says that we must "learn to make sense of" statements like "though the world does not change with a change of paradigm, the scientist afterward works in a different world." A consistent reading of that sentence requires that *world* be used in two different ways.

[28]Ibid., p. 113.

[29]Ibid., suggested on pp. 111, 114, 118.

[30]Ibid., p. 125. See also pp. 111-12.

[31]Ibid., pp. 121, 129, 150, for example.

[32]Ibid. See note 26; also Kuhn, "Reflections on My Critics," p. 270.

[33]Kuhn, *Structure of Scientific Revolutions,* for example, p. 103.

[34]Ibid., p. 47; also Kuhn, "Reflection on My Critics," pp. 267-68. See also Alan Musgrave, "Kuhn's Second Thoughts," in *Paradigms and Revolutions,* ed. Gary Gutting (Notre Dame: University of Notre Dame Press, 1980), pp. 39-53, reprinted from the *British Journal for the Philosophy of Science.*

[35]Kuhn, *Essential Tension,* p. 338; and Kuhn, "Reflections on My Critics," p. 266.

[36]Kuhn, *Structure of Scientific Revolutions,* p. 150.

[37]Ibid., for example, pp. 94, 122, 148, 150, 158; Kuhn, "Reflections on My Critics," p. 234; and Kuhn, *Essential Tension,* p. 332.

[38]Kuhn, *Structure of Scientific Revolutions,* pp. 122, 150.

[39]Ibid., for example, p. 150; and Kuhn, *Essential Tension,* p. 338.

[40]Kuhn, *Structure of Scientific Revolutions,* for example, p. 199; and especially Kuhn, *Essential Tensions,* chap. 13.

[41]Kuhn, *Essential Tensions,* p. 332.

[42]Kuhn, "Reflections on My Critics," pp. 234-35, 259-66.

[43]Kuhn, *Structure of Scientific Revolutions,* p. 170.

[44]Ibid., pp. 170-73, 206-7; and Kuhn, "Reflections on My Critics," pp. 264-66.

[45]Kuhn, *Structure of Scientific Revolutions,* p. 135.

[46]Ibid., p. 52, for example.

[47]Ibid., p. 206, for example.

[48]Ibid., pp. 121, 126.

[49]Kuhn, *Essential Tension,* chap. 13.

[50]See for example, Helen Longino, *Science as Social Knowledge* (Princeton, N.J.: Princeton University Press, 1977), p. 32, on this point.

[51]Some—for example, Michel Foucault—have included even those classified as insane in such groups *(Madness and Civilization,* pp. 288-89, quoted in David Cooper,

"Modern European Philosophy" in Nicholas Bunnin and E. P. Tsui-James, *The Blackwell Companion to Philosophy*, ed. [Cambridge, Mass.: Blackwell, 1996], p. 709).

[52]For example, David Hess, *Science Studies* (New York: New York University Press, 1977), p. 145. See also Sandra Harding, "After the Neutrality Ideal," in *The Problem of Western Science*, ed. Margaret C. Jacob (Atlantic Highlands, N.J.: Humanities Press, 1994), pp. 87, 94ff.

[53]Evelyn Keller, *Reflections on Gender and Science* (New Haven, Conn.: Yale, 1985), pp. 6-7, 131ff. See also her discussion of Nobel Prize biologist Barbara McClintock.

[54]See for example, ibid., pp. 162-67. Some more radical feminists hold that science does not need merely to be augmented by such resources but that male-dominated science will inevitably and inherently be pernicious and that it must be junked and replaced by a completely feminist science.

[55]See for example, Hess, *Science Studies*, p. 47. Also Steven Best, "Chaos and Entropy: Metaphors in Postmodern Science and Social Theory," *Science as Culture* 2.2, no. 11 (1991): 188-226.

[56]Putnam, *Reason, Truth and History*, pp. 134-37.

[57]Paul Feyerabend, *Against Method* (London: Verso, 1975), pp. 153-54.

[58]Ibid., p. 155.

[59]Ibid., pp. 155-56 (his emphasis).

[60]Brown, *Perception, Theory and Commitment*, p. 153.

[61]For instance, Donna Haraway: "[N]ature, at every level of the onion, is artefactual," quoted in Marcy Darnovsky, "Overhauling the Meaning Machines: An Interview with Donna Haraway," *Socialist Review* 21, no. 2 (1991): 82.

[62]See for example, Andrew Pickering, *Constructing Quarks* (Chicago: University of Chicago Press, 1984), p. 405; also Donna Haraway, *Primate Visions* (New York: Routledge, 1989), pp. 3-4.

[63]Bloor, *Knowledge and Social Imagery*, p. 87.

[64]Haraway, *Primate Visions*, p. 2; Hess, *Science Studies*, pp. 55, 121, 129.

[65]Longino, *Science as Social Knowledge*, 10ff.; Paul Gross and Norman Levitt, *The Higher Superstition* (Baltimore: Johns Hopkins, 1994, 1998), p. 49.

[66]The rejection is sweeping: "Postmodern social theory vigorously rejects every key axiom of modern philosophy and sociology. . . . Postmodernism . . . abandons all attempt to grasp totalities." Best, "Chaos and Entropy," pp. 195-96.

[67]Views in this neighborhood are held by, for example, Hans Georg Gadamer, *Truth and Method* (New York: Seabury, 1975), p. xxii, and Simone Weil, *Lectures on Philosophy* (New York: Cambridge, 1978), p. 70. See Cooper, "Modern European Philosophy," p. 713. The view that even the self may be a "'function' of language" is attributed by Cooper to Derrida (p. 717).

[68]See Longino, *Science as Social Knowledge*, p. 5. In this connection, Haraway claims that "There are people in the world . . . who really are *discursively* different, and that means *materially* different" (my emphasis) in Darnovsky, "Overhauling the Meaning Machines," p. 82. Gadamer explicitly rejects linguistic relativism, however.

[69]As John Searle puts the view (while decidedly not endorsing it), "we are always inside our own representations," *The Construction of Social Reality* (New York: Free Press, 1995), p. 172.

[70]Richard Rorty, *Objectivity, Relativism and Truth* (New York: Cambridge, 1991), p. 38.

[71]Longino, *Science as Social Knowledge,* pp. 10ff. Some see the implicit relativism as restricted. For instance, according to Sandra Harding, the position is

> not . . . that sciences are epistemologically relative to each and every culture's beliefs, such that all are equally defensible as true. Rather, the point is that they are historically relative to different cultures' *projects*—to cultures' questions about the natural and social order. Different questions produce different answers containing distinctive, sometimes conflicting, representations of nature and, indeed, of science, and the representations that conflict do not fit together like pieces of a jigsaw puzzle.

Harding, "Science Is Good to Think With," in *Science Wars,* ed. Andrew Ross (Durham, N.C.: Duke University Press, 1996), p. 17.

[72]Some (e.g., Haraway), seem to feel that their views undercut mainstream science so fundamentally that one can properly dismiss it without coming to grips with it. That, at least, is the interpretation of Gross and Levitt, *The Higher Superstition,* p. 130.

[73]Best, "Chaos and Entropy," p. 204.

[74]This view of science simply as power grows in part out of postmodern appropriation of Nietzsche.

[75]Stanley Aronowitz, *Science as Power* (Minneapolis: University of Minnesota Press, 1988).

[76]For such views, see for example, Keller, *Reflections on Gender and Science,* pp. 6-7, 10; Harding, "After the Neutrality Ideal," pp. 82, 88.

[77]Haraway, *Primate Visions,* p. 4.

[78]Andrew Ross, *Strange Weather* (London: Verso, 1991), p. 29. Ross even claims that one aim of the movement is "to see science redeem its tarnished ideals" (Ross, *Science Wars,* p. 11).

[79]Haraway, *Primate Visions,* pp. 3, 4. Indeed, for Haraway, facts have a "politically contested nature."

[80]Pickering, *Constructing Quarks,* pp. 413-14.

[81]Rorty, *Objectivity, Relativism and Truth,* p. 38.

[82]Some postmodernists also deny that science makes *progress.* What, then, is it to make a scientific discovery? The view of some (e.g., Lyotard) would imply that it is merely being the first to make a particular linguistic play that is recognized as scoring approval-points in the context of the rules of a particular type of discursive game (science).

[83]The list here stretches from Darwin himself to, for example, Haldane, and to various Nazi physicists. Except in the latter case, most were apparently just well-intentioned representative products of their times and cultures.

[84]This constitutes the main thrust of Gross and Levitt's *The Higher Superstition,* who employ such phrases as "vaporous pontification," "philosophical styrofoam," etc.

[85]For extended criticism and useful discussion see Frederick Suppe, ed., *The Structure of Scientific Theories* (Urbana: University of Illinois, 1977); and W. H. Newton-Smith, *Rationality of Science* (Boston: Routledge and Kegan Paul, 1981).

[86]This is Kuhn's own point in *Essential Tension,* p. 235.

[87]See Suppe, *Structure of Scientific Theories,* pp. 633-49.

[88]For instance, Dudley Shapere, "The Structure of Scientific Revolutions," *Philosophical Review* 73 (1964): 383-94, reprinted in *Paradigms and Revolutions,* ed. Gutting, pp.

27-38. Also widely cited on this issue is Margaret Masterson, "The Nature of a Paradigm," in *Criticism and the Growth of Knowledge,* ed. Lakatos and Musgrave, pp. 59-90.

[89]Suppe, *Structure of Scientific Theories,* p. 648. Suppe lists a number of additional references on this same point.

[90]For further discussion of the following plus other criticism of Kuhn, see ibid., pp. 633-49; Newton-Smith, *Rationality of Science,* pp. 102-24; Larry Laudan, *Progress and Its Problems* (Berkeley: University of California Press, 1977), pp. 73-76; and essays in Lakatos and Musgrave, eds., *Criticism and the Growth of Knowledge.* There is currently quite a large critical literature.

[91]See, for example, the essays of Shapere and Musgrave in *Paradigms and Revolutions.* See also Putnam, *Reason, Truth and History,* pp. 114-16. There is quite a large literature on this topic.

[92]See especially Ernan McMullin, "Values in Science," *Proceedings of the Biennial Meeting of the Philosophy of Science Association* 2 (1982): 1-25.

[93]For this particular discussion I am heavily indebted to Professor Stephen Wykstra.

Chapter 4. The Contemporary Situation

[1]Imre Lakatos, "Falsification and the Methodology of Scientific Research Programmes," in *Criticism and the Growth of Knowledge,* ed. Imre Lakatos and Alan Musgrave (Cambridge: Cambridge University Press, 1970); and Larry Laudan, *Progress and Its Problems* (Berkley: University of California Press, 1977).

[2]This point is from Professor Stephen Wykstra.

[3]See for example, Dudley Shapere, "Scientific Theories and Their Domains," in *The Structure of Scientific Theories,* ed. Frederick Suppe (Urbana: University of Illinois Press, 1977); and also Suppe's own remarks in response to Shapere, for example, p. 573.

[4]Jerry Fodor, "Observation Reconsidered," *Philosophy of Science* 51, no. 1 (March 1984): 23-43. The point concerning illusions is also his. See also Robert Causey, "Theory and Observation," in *Current Research in Philosophy of Science,* ed. Peter Asquith and Henry Kyburg Jr. (Ann Arbor, Mich.: Edwards Brothers, 1971), pp. 187-206.

[5]See W. H. Newton-Smith, *The Rationality of Science* (Boston: Routledge and Kegan Paul, 1981), p. 211, for example. Much of his book is relevant to this section.

[6]For general discussion of this area see Alvin Plantinga and Nicholas Wolterstorff, eds., *Faith and Rationality* (Notre Dame: University of Notre Dame Press, 1983), especially part 4 B of Plantinga's essay "Reason and Belief in God" and sections 5-12 of Wolterstorff's essay "Can Belief in God Be Rational If It Has No Foundations?" The position outlined there and in the present paragraph is basically Reidian, after the eighteenth-century Scottish Common Sense philosopher Thomas Reid. See also Mary Stewart Van Leeuwen, *The Sorcerer's Apprentice* (Downers Grove, Ill.: InterVarsity Press, 1982), chaps. 1 and 2; and C. Stephen Evans, *Preserving the Person* (Grand Rapids, Mich.: Baker, 1982), chap. 4.

[7]See Ernan McMullin, "Values in Science," *Proceedings of the Biennial Meeting of the Philosophy of Science Association* 2 (1982): 1-25.

[8]Thomas Kuhn, *The Essential Tension* (Chicago: University of Chicago Press, 1997), pp. 331-32.

[9]Ibid., pp. 321-22.
[10]Ibid., p. 335.
[11]Ibid., p. 332.
[12]For example, Suppe, *Structure of Scientific Theories*, p. 652. Suppe takes the emerging trend in philosophy of science to be "historical realism."
[13]Ibid., p. 336. See also Newton-Smith, *Rationality of Science*, p. 270 and pp. 221-23, 259.
[14]An interesting discussion is to be found in Newton-Smith, *Rationality of Science*, pp. 256-57. But see also pp. 210-15.

Chapter 5. The Competence of Science

[1]This definition owes much to Professor Alvin Plantinga—or at least I do.
[2]For discussion, see Mary Hesse, "Models and Analogy in Science," in *The Encyclopedia of Philosophy,* ed. Paul Edwards (New York: Macmillan, 1967). The first view mentioned (no model) is often associated with Pierre Duhem, the second with N. R. Campbell.
[3]This typology of antirealist views was suggested by Professor Alvin Plantinga. See also his "How to Be an Anti-realist," *Proceedings and Addresses of the American Philosophical Association* 56, no. 1 (September 1982): 47-70.
[4]Bertrand Russell seems to have held some version of this.
[5]Operationism is generally associated with the American physicist P. W. Bridgeman.
[6]This I take to be the view of Bas Van Fraassen, in *The Scientific Image* (Oxford: Oxford University Press, 1980).
[7]In this connection see also William Hasker, *Metaphysics* (Downers Grove, Ill.: Inter-Varsity Press, 1983), chap. 4.
[8]For example, Fritz Rohrlich and Larry Hardin, "Established Theories," *Philosophy of Science* 50, no. 4 (December 1983): 603-17.
[9]See for example, Mary Hesse, "The Explanatory Function of Metaphor," *Revolutions and Reconstructions in the Philosophy of Science* (Bloomington: Indiana University Press, 1980).
[10]See W. H. Newton-Smith, "The Thesis of Verisimilitude," in *The Rationality of Science* (Boston: Routledge and Kegan Paul, 1981).
[11]The first part of this section (on the confirmation of correspondence rules) has been heavily influenced by the work of Clark Glymour. The view developed is essentially Glymour's "bootstrapping" conception found in his *Theory and Evidence* (Princeton, N.J.: Princeton University Press, 1980), esp. chap. 5.
[12]Ibid.
[13]Newton-Smith, *Rationality of Science*, pp. 226-32. See also Ernan McMullin, "Values in Science," *Proceedings of the Biennial Meeting of the Philosophy of Science Association* 2 (1982): 13-14.
[14]Newton-Smith, *Rationality of Science*, p. 196.
[15]For example, Frederick Suppe, ed. *The Structure of Scientific Theories* (Urbana: University of Illnois Press, 1977), p. 652. Again, Suppe takes the emerging trend in philosophy of science to be "historical realism."

Chapter 6. The Limitations of Science

[1]See W. H. Newton-Smith, *The Rationality of Science* (Boston: Routledge and Kegan

Paul, 1981) p. 270; Thomas Kuhn, *The Essential Tension* (Chicago: University of Chicago Press, 1997), p. 336; and Ernan McMullin, "Values in Science," *Proceedings of the Biennial Meeting of the Philosophy of Science Association* 2 (1982): 20-21.

[2]Edward Tryon, quoted in *Science Digest,* June 1984, p. 101.

[3]See note 3, chap. 3.

[4]For example, Ruth Benedict, "Anthropology and the Abnormal," *Journal of General Psychology* 10 (1934): 59-80, reprinted in part in William Alston and Richard Brandt, eds., *The Problems of Philosophy* (Boston: Allyn and Bacon, 1974), pp. 143-49.

[5]Arthur Holmes makes a similar point in *Ethics* (Downers Grove, Ill.: InterVarsity Press, 1984), p. 20.

Chapter 7. "Scientific" Challenges to Religious Belief

[1]Some remarks here were suggested by Alvin Plantinga's essay in *Faith and Rationality,* ed. Alvin Plantinga and Nicholas Wolterstorff (Notre Dame: University of Notre Dame Press, 1983).

[2]Some remarks of Plantinga (ibid.) are also relevant here.

[3]Again Plantinga's work suggested this.

Chapter 8. Design & Science

[1]It can be seen in the background and sometimes in the forefront of the scientific work of such majors figures as Newton, Boyle, Descartes and—later—Pasteur, Herschel, Faraday, Maxwell and others.

[2]The replica garbage heap would be deliberately produced *in accord with an idea* and might be said in that sense to be designed. But the idea itself would not embody design in the more fundamental sense of resonating with mind. The isomorphisms (the match) between the original and the replica *would* exemplify such a resonance, and that is why the term *design* would be derivatively appropriate in this case. The Martian Stonehenge replica would exhibit designedness in *both* senses.

[3]That was the form of the initial alien communication in the movie *Contact.* SETI actually looks for signals of two sorts. Nearly any high-tech civilization is presumed to produce *unintentional* electromagnetic radiation (e.g., byproduct radiation from operation of electronic equipment, from communication systems, from manufacturing processes, etc.), and SETI looks for that kind of signal as well as for deliberately patterned signals. Either type of signal would constitute an *artifact,* but the former would not represent *design.*

[4]I am not suggesting that this sort of pattern is the only type relevant to designedness. Indeed, I think that there are several different, entire categories of pattern that are relevant. The present sort, involving obvious cognitive content, is simply the most intuitively easy to identify.

[5]Of course, it can work the other way too. When Jocelyn Bell detected the first of what later came to be known as pulsars, there were no known or even suspected mechanisms by which nature could produce such pulsed signals, and the source was informally named "LGM-1"—for Little Green Men 1.

[6]This general sort of view with respect to creationism is explicitly endorsed by, for example, Douglas Futuyma, Michael Ruse and others.

[7]I have been employing the concept of *intervention* here, but some Christians believe

that the entire idea of intervention is a bit off target. For instance, it is possible that what we identify as statements of natural laws are actually just descriptions of God's free but perfectly consistent activity, and that there simply are no independent "natural" regularities that those actions are interventions into or contraventions of. (For some technical exploration of that idea, see Del Ratzsch, "Nomo(theo)logical Necessity," in *Faith and Philosophy* 4 [1987]: 383-402.) Or it is possible that there are genuine background "natural" regularities but that God intervenes in various perfectly consistent, uniform ways in specific circumstances, so that at least *some* of the uniformities we identify as natural laws actually consist of specific supernatural activity. In the former case, and perhaps to some extent in the latter case, talk of "intervention" would be in some circumstances misdirected.

[8]For instance, Eugenie Scott says: "To be dealt with scientifically, 'intelligence' must be natural because *all* science is natural. . . . SETI is indeed a scientific project; it seeks *natural* intelligence." *NCSE Reports* 10, no. 1 (January-February 1990): 16-18.

[9]Among those holding all or part of that view are Fred Hoyle, Chandra Wickramesingh and the codiscoverer of DNA, Francis Crick.

[10]Philosophical naturalism is basically the view that the natural realm is the only reality there is and that science is the only access we have to the fundamental structures and principles defining and governing that reality. There are some Christian advocates of methodological naturalism who object to the above characterization of *methodological naturalism* as "doing science as *if* philosophical naturalism were true." But their objections seem to me to be primarily that the definition makes no mention of God upholding all created things in such a way that were that support withdrawn all those things would collapse into nonexistence, no mention that the laws and character of created things are as they are because God chose to make things that way, etc.—all things that many Christian methodological naturalists affirm. Those are indeed important differences from philosophical naturalism. Nonetheless, given what most methodological naturalists mean by "science," the expectation would be that a properly pursued methodological naturalist *science* and a properly pursued philosophical naturalist *science* would be identical—containing the same laws, principles, theories, data, methods and so forth. It is in that sense that the characterization I give of methodological naturalism is, I think, accurate.

[11]Some early figures—for example, Leibniz—took this sort of position as *theologically* preferable to intervention views.

[12]For instance, Dugald Stewart, in his 1792 *Elements of the Philosophy of the Human Mind* 1:52, says: "In the investigation of physical laws, it is well-known that our inquiries must always terminate in some general fact, of which no account can be given, but that such is the constitution of nature. After we have established, for example, from the astronomical phenomena, the universality of the law of gravitation, it may still be asked whether this law implies the constant agency of mind; and (upon the supposition that it does) whether it be probable that the Diety always operates immediately, or by means of subordinate instruments? But these questions, however curious, do not fall under the province of the natural philosopher [scientist]. It is sufficient for his purpose, if the universality of the fact be admitted."

[13]Indeed, the apparent possibility of virtually *anything* having empirical consequences

when conjoined with suitably constructed bridge principles posed difficulties for some key doctrines of positivism.

[14]Paul Davies, *Are We Alone?* (New York: Basic, 1995), p. 138.

[15]Such arguments are contained in various of the *Bridgewater Treatises,* notably Whewell's and Chalmers's. Of course, some design arguments did rest quite explicitly upon gaps—see, for example, Bell's *Bridgewater Treatise.* A variety of non-gap arguments—all from scientists—can be found in Francis Mason, ed., *The Great Design* (1934; reprint, Freeport, N.Y.: Books for Libraries, 1972). Such arguments can also be found in works not usually associated with design cases—for example, Faraday's. See David Gooding, "Metaphysics Versus Measurement: The Conversion and Conservation of Force in Faraday's Physics," *Annals of Science* 37 (1980): 29.

[16]For instance, in *A Free Inquiry into the Vulgarly Received Notions of Nature* (1685-86), Boyle says: "It much more tends to the illustration of God's wisdom, to have framed things at first, that there can seldom or never need any extraordinary interposition of his power. And, as it more recommends the skill of an engineer to contrive an elaborate engine so, as that there should need nothing to reach his ends in it but the contrivance of parts devoid of understanding, than if it were necessary, that ever and anon, a discreet servant should be employed to concur notably to the operation of this or that part, or to hinder the engine from being out of order; so it more sets off the wisdom of God in the fabric of the universe that he can make so vast a machine perform all those many things, which he designed it should, by the mere contrivance of brute matter managed by certain laws of local motion and upheld by his ordinary and general concourse, than if he employed from time to time an intelligent overseer, such as nature is fancied to be, to regulate, and control the motions of the parts." (Marie Hall, ed., *Robert Boyle on Natural Philosophy* [Bloomington: Indiana University Press, 1965, 1966], pp. 150-51). Similar sentiments can be found in Boyle's *The Excellency of Theology, Compared with Natural Philosophy,* in Hall, *Robert Boyle on Natural Philosophy,* pp. 140-41.

[17]And the common conception that historically the move among Christian scientists from locating design in gaps to locating design in laws was a desperate retreat in the face of Darwin is simply myth. That *type* of move long predated Darwin.

[18]One additional interesting consideration is that although science may have an impressive record of closing gaps, it has a nearly equally distinguished record of opening new gaps. Every unsolved scientific puzzle represents a (perhaps very temporary) explanatory gap in our science—if it were not, it would not be a puzzle. New theories that solve such puzzles—and thus close the gaps in question—typically open new lines of research. Indeed, some philosophers of science think that it is one criterion of a good theory that it suggest new research. But those new lines of research nearly invariably generate new puzzles. Thus scientific advances *themselves* frequently generate (or at least uncover) new gaps in our scientific understanding of the world. And every explanatory gap in our science is potentially a gap in the causal structure of the purely natural world. Historically science may have opened as many gaps as it has closed.

[19]Of course, design arguments that do not involve gaps do not even in principle offer explanatory shortcuts, since in such cases there will still be a full immediate causal explanation of the production of the characteristics constituting evidence of design.

[20]As Sir Oliver Lodge remarked: "If we have to postulate a spiritual world at all, we may

as well utilize it throughout; not appealing to it unnecessarily, seeking always a proximate explanation; holding on to physics as far as we possible can, but being ready to abandon it whenever its methods are seen to be entirely incompetent" ("Design and Purpose in the Universe," in *The Great Design,* ed. Francis Mason [New York: Macmillan, 1934], p. 228). Later in the same paragraph Lodge explicitly includes design in nature in the relevant category.

[21]Among the latter are strong anthropic principles, participatory anthropic principles and many worlds hypotheses.

[22]The work of Phillip Johnson, who is the acknowledged leader of the ID group, constitutes the most visible statement of the ID movement on this issue.

[23]Various people in this group do not explicitly identify the designer of the design in nature as God and have consequently been accused of disingenuousness. However, given the legitimate separability of issues of design, the character of design evidence, identification of designedness and so forth from questions concerning the identity of the designer in question, such accusations seem misguided. The former questions can in fact be investigated independently of the latter. It is true, however, that nearly every member of the movement does believe that design in nature would ultimately track back to God.

[24]It is generally claimed both that biochemical data have undergone revolutionary changes making design vastly more plausible, and that alternative explanations (e.g., of origins of life, based on Miller-Urey results, etc.) have during the same time been increasingly exposed as unworkable.

[25]The complexity in question is "irreducible" complexity, the probability involves "specification" of a certain sort, and the information in question is that of Shannon information theory. For complexity arguments see Michael Behe, *Darwin's Black Box* (New York: Free Press, 1996). For improbability arguments, see William A. Dembski, *The Design Inference* (New York: Cambridge University Press, 1998). Information arguments occur in quite a number of places, from, for example, Thaxton, Bradley and Olson, to Wilder-Smith.

[26]Michael Behe, author of *Darwin's Black Box,* specifically denies any hostility toward common descent of all species.

[27]Ironically, such underestimating of nature can also have roots in overestimations of science—for example, implicitly assuming that if *our science* cannot explain something, and thus tacitly identifies it as a gap, then it really *is* a gap, and nature cannot have the requisite capabilities to bridge it.

[28]There are a number of scientists—both Christian and non-Christian—who suspect that to be the case.

[29]The theories of, for example, Stuart Kauffman, Rupert Sheldrake and others constitute attempts to uncover the outlines of previously unsuspected capacities of nature.

Chapter 9. Christianity & Scientific Pursuits
[1]Genesis 2:15.

[2]Genesis 1:28.

[3]For example, Bernard Ramm, *The Christian View of Science and Scripture* (London: Paternoster, 1955), p. 25.

[4]For example, Genesis 1:31. See also Philippians 4:8.

[5]A number of points in this section were suggested by remarks of Professor Alvin Plantinga.

[6]"In discovering the secret of man's lowly origin Darwin had lost confidence in the power of human reason and intuition to penetrate the riddle of the universe. He had, he confessed, an 'inward conviction' that the universe was not the result of mere chance. 'But then,' he added, 'with me the horrid doubt always arises whether the convictions of man's mind, which has been developed from the mind of the lower animals, are of any value or at all trustworthy. Would anyone trust in the convictions of a monkey's mind, if there are any convictions in such a mind?'" (John C. Greene, *The Death of Adam* [Ames: Iowa State University Press, 1959], p. 336). The inner quotes are from a letter of Darwin's to William Graham, Down, July 3, 1881, taken from Francis Darwin, ed., *The Life and Letters of Charles Darwin Including an Autobiographical Chapter* (New York: n.p., 1898), 1:285.

[7]This from Professor Nicholas Wolterstorff. Abraham Kuyper held that to do good science one had to have a "seeking sympathy" toward nature.

Chapter 10. Christianity & the Specific Content of Science

[1]David Dye, in *Faith and the Physical World* (Grand Rapids, Mich.: Eerdmans, 1966), comes quite close to this position (see, e.g., pp. 51, 69). His conception of science has much in common with the positivist view. Rudolf Bultmann may fit into this category as well.

[2]The general notion of complementarity is more ancient than is sometimes realized. For instance, consider the following statement of a complementarist-style position: "And yet, in my opinion, it is no absurdity to say that they were both in the right, both natural philosopher and diviner, one justly detecting the cause of this event, by which it was produced, the other the end for which it was designed. For it was the business of the one to find out and give an account of what it was made, and in what manner and by what means it grew as it did; and of the other to foretell to what end and purpose it was so made, and what it might mean or portend. Those who say that to find out the cause of a prodigy is in effect to destroy its supposed signification as such, do not take notice, that, at the same time, together with divine prodigies, they also do away with signs and signals of human art and concert, as, for instance, the clashing of quoits, fire-beacons, and the shadows of sun-dials, every one of which has its cause, and by that cause and contrivance is a sign of something else. But these are subjects, perhaps, that would better befit another place" (Plutarch's *Lives,* trans. John Dryden [New York: Modern Library], p. 186 [the life of Pericles]). Plutarch's dates were somewhere around A.D. 45-120. Notice, incidentally, that the explanatory examples are taken from means of human communications, which are exactly the sort employed by contemporary complementarists. This passage was pointed out to me by Professor David Van Baak.

[3]There may be no consistent strict complementarist, but a good candidate is Richard Bube, *The Human Quest* (Waco, Tex.: Word, 1971). Remarks on pages 50 and 55 tend in this direction, but the case is not decisive. Perhaps the best-known complementarist is Donald MacKay, for example, *The Clockwork Image* (Downers Grove, Ill.: InterVarsity Press, 1974), but the case for his being a *strict* complementarist is equivocal.

[4]For example, Bube, *Human Quest,* p. 35.

[5]MacKay, *Clockwork Image,* pp. 78-81; and also his *Science and the Quest for Meaning* (Grand Rapids, Mich.: Eerdmans, 1982), pp. 22-28. Complementarists have in the past attempted to salvage this particular separation of freedom and determinism by proposing various definitions of what *freedom* means. The best known attempt (MacKay) defines freedom in terms of law-based predictions of one's states (and actions) which have "unconditional claim" to one's assent. The argument is that if one *believed* such a prediction or description, that very belief would change the original initial conditions employed in the prediction, and thus the prediction would simply not apply. Hence, one would be correct in not believing the prediction, and the prediction would thus not have unconditional claim to one's assent. All of that is correct, but it is not clear what it has to do with freedom. The fact that deterministic predictions can vary with varying initial conditions does not say anything about determinism or freedom and certainly does not show their compatibility, even if they are claimed to hold on different levels, unless one just stipulates that that is what freedom means. It is far from obvious that such a definition comes close to what we typically mean by *freedom,* however.

[6]MacKay seems to recognize this (e.g., he speaks of having to discover what phenomena on one level "correlate" with those on another—*Clockwork Image,* pp. 44, 93), which is why I hesitate to term him a strict complementarist.

[7]For example, Robert L. Reymond, *A Christian View of Modern Science* (Nutley, N.J.: Presbyterian & Reformed, 1977). The claim that the effects of Christian belief extend even to 2 and 2 being 4 is his, p. 29. Cornelius Van Til and Herman Dooyeweerd are widely interpreted as fitting into this category as well.

[8]This seems to be the view in Nicholas Wolterstorff, *Reason Within the Bounds of Religion* (Grand Rapids, Mich.: Eerdmans, 1976); and Abraham Kuyper, *Principles of Sacred Theology* (1894; reprint, Grand Rapids, Mich.: Baker, 1980). Some secular philosophers of science, for example, Larry Laudan, take similar positions.

[9]For example, Kuyper, *Principles of Sacred Theology,* pp. 159-220, passim.

[10]This is *perhaps* the category MacKay belongs in.

[11]Many critics of creationism base some of their criticisms on this type of view. See, for instance, Niles Eldredge, *The Monkey Business* (New York: Washington Square Press, 1982), pp. 10, 134, 146.

[12]Discussion relevant to this position is found in Ernan McMullin, "How Should Cosmology Relate to Theology?" in *The Sciences and Theology in the Twentieth Century,* ed. A. R. Peacocke (Notre Dame, Ind.: University of Notre Dame Press, 1981).

[13]I believe that this view is held by, for example, Professor John Stek.

[14]For instance, Henry Morris, *Studies in the Bible and Science* (Philadelphia: Presbyterian & Reformed, 1966). Several of the essays included in the book are relevant.

[15]For instance, Roland Mushat Frye, "Creation-Science Against the Religious Background," from *Is God a Creationist?* (New York: Scribners, 1983), pp. 1-28. Frye says, "The various biblical references to creation are magnificent descriptions, sublime in their symbolic vision, inspiring in their religious faith, but there is simply no way that we can derive from them a single, literal 'creation-science.' Nor should we. Their frame of reference is different" (p. 14). Frye's piece has also been published separately (slightly edited) as "The Religious Case Against Creation-Science" (report 1 from the Center for Theological Inquiry, Princeton, New Jersey, 1983).

[16]"Accommodation" views—the idea that God accommodated his message to the language, concepts and ideas already available to its recipients—fall in this general area, as do Bultmann's contentions that we have to strip away the outmoded cultural wrappings of Scripture, or, as he says, "demythologize" Scripture.

[17]Henry Morris is generally put in this category. His method of interpreting Scripture is not, however, as oversimple as it is sometimes portrayed. For instance, in Henry Morris, "The Bible and Theistic Evolution," *Studies in the Bible and Science,* pp. 89-93, one can extract at least six interpretive principles relating to the question of *when* a passage of Scripture ought to be taken literally.

[18]For instance, R. L. Wysong, *The Creation-Evolution Controversy* (Midland, Mich.: Inquiry Press, 1976), p. 40, employs the following definition of *science,* which he takes from the Oxford dictionary: "A branch of study which is concerned either with a connected body of *demonstrated truths* or with *observed facts* systematically classified and more or less colligated and brought under general laws, and which includes trustworthy methods for the discovery of new truth within its own domain" (Wysong's emphasis). Morris and Gish use similar (sometimes identical) definitions and sometimes add that science cannot deal with processes not *presently* observable. Besides exhibiting the positivistic conception of science that many creationists work with, the above also demonstrates the hazards of employing a commercial dictionary as a source of philosophical information. Oddly enough, some of the creationists' critics employ similar conceptions of science. See, for instance, an analysis of the Overton decision (Arkansas creation/evolution trial) by Larry Laudan, "Science at the Bar: Causes for Concern," reprinted as appendix B, pp. 149-54 in Jeffrie G. Murphy, *Evolution, Morality and the Meaning of Life* (Totowa, N.J.: Rowman and Littlefield, 1982). Also of interest in this respect among critics of creationism is the official pronouncement of the National Academy of Science on creationism, *Science and Creationism* (Washington, D.C.: National Academy Press, 1984). Their position seems to be based on a naive reading of Popper (see especially pp. 8-11). And despite listing "the nature of science" as first on their list of "five central scientific issues" of relevance (as if the nature of science were itself a scientific issue), the committee of eleven who produced the statement contains no philosophers of science (four people who are apparently lawyers, though), and the statement lists nothing in philosophy of science among its references, and only one such work among "other publications of interest." For much more extensive discussion of this general topic, see Del Ratzsch, *The Battle of Beginnings* (Downers Grove, Ill.: InterVarsity Press, 1996), chaps. 10 and 11.

[19]This is the general area of "concordist" views subscribed to, to some extent, by Davis Young, Robert Fisher and Bernard Ramm (who calls his own view, as developed in *The Christian View of Science and Scripture,* "moderate concordism"). We also get this view explicitly in Hugh Ross, *Genesis One: A Scientific Perspective* (Sierra Madre: Wiseman, 1979).

[20]Ross, *Genesis One,* p. 16: "Most Bible scholars (and scientists too) would agree that a correct, or 'literal,' interpretation of the creation 'day' is one that takes into account definitions, context, grammar, and relevant passages from other parts of scripture. A careful analysis of all these elements yields the following reasons for literally interpreting the creation days of Genesis as long periods of time."

[21]For example, Abraham Kuyper, *Lectures on Calvinism* (1898; reprint, Grand Rapids, Mich.: Eerdmans, 1978), pp. 114-15, 197.

Appendix

[1]*Liberalism,* as Huxley used the term, involved philosophical naturalism and included the view that "religion is an emotionally valid form of human experience, but *false when formalized into statement about objective reality*" (my emphasis). See, for example, Ruth Barton, *The X Club: Science, Religion, and Social Change in Victorian England* (University Microfilms: Ph.D. dissertation, University of Pennsylvania, 1976), pp. 72-74.

[2]For the original statement, see "NABT Unveils New Statement of Teaching Evolution," *NCSE Reports* 17, no. 1 (January-February 1997): 31-32. For a brief account of the modification, see Eugenie C. Scott, "NABT Statement on Evolution Evolves," *NCSE Reports* 17, no. 4 (July-August 1997): 4-5.

[3]In a recent article about the commercial market in dinosaur (and other) fossils, one dealer explained the popularity of such fossils in extremely telling terms:

> [Since there is a limited supply of such fossils] people think, "Maybe I should grab it before it's too late." . . . Museums can't satisfy the public's demand now. Just look at this dinosaur egg. There's a power in it. It's real, more real than any man-made thing. The egg is a direct link to evolution, to Darwin and *Jurassic Park.* It's like owning a piece of the cross.

(Henry Galiano, quoted in Virginia Morell, "A Dinosaur for the Mantel," *Natural History* [October 1998]: 64.)

[4]Richard Dawkins, *The Blind Watchmaker* (N.Y.: Norton, 1987), p. 6.

[5]Thomas Nagel, *The Last Word* (New York: Oxford, 1997), p. 131.

[6]Paul Tillich, *Dynamics of Faith* (New York: Harper, 1956, 1957), p. 81.

[7]In this general connection see Del Ratzch, *The Battle of Beginnings* (Downers Grove, Ill.: InterVarsity Press, 1996), especially chap. 11.

[8]Not only creationist popularizers, but a number of the most influential professional creationists in the U.S. explicitly adopt that definition. See footnote 18, chap. 10.

[9]For more detail, see Ratzsch, *Battle of Beginnings,* chap. 10.

[10]The foregoing is just one example. See Ratzsch, *Battle of Beginnings,* chap. 4, for further discussion.

Further Reading

The following list is quite incomplete. Readers are urged to consult other works referred to in the text.

Traditional Views, Advocates

Hempel, Carl. *The Philosophy of Natural Science*. Englewood Cliffs, N.J.: Prentice-Hall, 1966.

Nagel, Ernest. *The Structure of Science*. New York: Harcourt, Brace and World, 1961.

The Hempel book is quite readable, the Nagel more technical.

Kuhnian and Radical Views, Advocates

Bloor, David. *Knowledge and Social Imagery*. Boston: Routledge and Kegan Paul, 1976.

Brown, Harold I. *Perception, Theory and Commitment*. Chicago: University of Chicago Press, 1977.

Feyerabend, Paul. *Against Method*. London: Verso Edition, 1975.

Hess, David. *Science Studies: An Advanced Introduction*. New York: New York University Press, 1977.

Keller, Evelyn Fox. *Reflections on Gender and Science*. New Haven, Conn.: Yale University Press, 1985.

Kuhn, Thomas. *The Structure of Scientific Revolutions*. Chicago: University of Chicago Press, 1962.

Lakatos, Imre. "Falsification and the Methodology of Scientific Research Programmes." In *Criticism and the Growth of Knowledge*. Edited by Imre Lakatos and Alan Musgrave. Cambridge: Cambridge University Press, 1970.

Longino, Helen. *Science as Social Knowledge*. Princeton: Princeton University Press, 1990.

Kuhn and Brown are quite readable (minor technicalities in Brown), Bloor and Feyerabend are a bit more difficult, and Lakatos is more technical yet. Hess is a survey of current (often controversial) interdisciplinary study of science itself. Keller and Longino represent sensible approaches with feminist sympathies.

Surveys/Critical Evaluations of the Above Views

Chalmers, A. F. *What Is This Thing Called Science?* St. Lucia, Queensland: University of Queensland Press, 1976.

Newton-Smith, W. H. *The Rationality of Science.* Boston: Routledge and Kegan Paul, 1981.

Suppe, Frederick. *The Structure of Scientific Theories.* Urbana: University of Illinois Press, 1977.

Newton-Smith and Chalmers are both wide ranging and readable, but I recommend the Newton-Smith. Suppe is the most detailed, the most technical and the most difficult to read. Criticisms of the traditional and positivist views can be found in almost all works written by Kuhnians and radicals, since they are typically reacting against those earlier views. Brown (above) contains some especially nice criticisms of that sort.

Contemporary Views

Gale, George. *Theory of Science.* New York: McGraw-Hill, 1971.

Glymour, Clark. *Theory and Evidence.* Princeton: Princeton University Press, 1981.

Laudan, Larry. *Progress and Its Problems.* Berkeley: University of California Press, 1977.

Van Fraassen, Bas. *The Scientific Image.* Oxford: Clarendon Press, 1980.

Glymour and Gale are realists, Van Fraassen and Laudan nonrealists. Laudan and Gale are less technical, Glymour and Van Fraassen more technical. Laudan also has some more recent books in print. Newton-Smith (realist) is recommended here as well, as are a number of separate articles by Ernan McMullin (see notes).

Design

Behe, Michael. *Darwin's Black Box.* New York: Free Press, 1996.

Dembski, William. *The Design Inference.* Cambridge: Cambridge University Press, 1998.

Dembski, William, ed. *Mere Creation: Science, Faith and Intelligent Design.* Downers Grove, Ill.: InterVarsity Press, 1998

Moreland, J. P., ed. *The Creation Hypothesis.* Downers Grove, Ill.: InterVarsity Press, 1994.

Science and Christianity

Readers are directed to authors cited in the notes for chapters 9 and 10 although by no means are the views of all those authors endorsed. Those authors include Bernard Ramm, David Dye, Richard Bube, Donald MacKay, Robert Reymond, Nicholas Wolterstorff, Abraham Kuyper, Ernan McMullin, Henry Morris, Roland Mushat Frye, Davis Young and Robert Fischer. That list represents only the tip of the iceberg. Ramm, Bube and MacKay have probably been the most influential among Christian scientists. Morris has been quite influential among laypeople. Kuyper and Wolterstorff have been influential in Reformed circles. Also widely read are J. P. Moreland, Nancey Murphy, Mary Midgley, John Polkinghorne, R. Hooykaas, Eugene Klaarens, Stanley Jaki, Thomas Torrance, Howard Van Till and Ian Barbour. A number of periodicals such as *Perspectives* and *Christian Scholar's Review* publish articles in this area. The journals and their articles vary in quality and theology, as do the books in this area.

Index